LEGACY CHURCHES

Stephen Gray
and
Franklin Dumond

ChurchSmart
RESOURCES

St. Charles, IL 60174
1-800-253-4276

ChurchSmart RESOURCES

Published by ChurchSmart Resources

We are an evangelical Christian publisher committed to producing excellent products at affordable prices to help church leaders accomplish effective ministry in the areas of Church planting, Church growth, Church renewal and Leadership development.

For a free catalog of our resources call 1-800-253-4276.
Visit us at: *www.churchsmart.com*

Cover design by: Julie Becker

ISBN-10: 1-889638-78-1
ISBN-13: 978-1-889638-78-2

LEGACY CHURCHES

ENDORSEMENTS

Legacy Churches is a dangerous and challenging call to rethink what it means to invest in the life of the local church. Stephen Gray and Franklin Dumond use real life stories and up-to-date statistics to describe churches that are interested in doing more than keeping the doors open. This book describes legacy-leaving churches that reproduce new churches, even if it requires closing the doors of the original church. I highly recommend *Legacy Churches*. It is an asset to any pastor or denominational leader who desires to leave a lasting legacy beyond one single local church.
— Dr. Derek Vreeland, Pastor, Cornerstone Church, Americus, Georgia

Sometimes good medicine is strong medicine. Leaving a legacy is both good and strong. If your congregation is wondering what to do next, you should read this book carefully and prayerfully. The second half of the book will help guide you through the next steps with excellent diagnostic tools and practical clear instructions. This is a must read for every congregation older than 25 years.
— Marcus Bigelow, West Regional Director, President at Large of STADIA

"Stephen Gray has done it again! After releasing his great book, *Planting Fast Growing Churches* to help church planters, he, along with Dr. Franklin Dumond has gone to the next level to help churches that want to leave a legacy after they are gone. The self-test on page 80 and the even more important issues it helps a legacy church begin to talk about is worth the price of the entire book. These men are some of the best church consultants I know. If the readers of this book will pray for God's wisdom and put the principles of this book into practice, all heaven will party and the Kingdom will keep expanding!
— Dr. Larry McKain, Executive Director of New Church Specialties

Drs. Gray and Dumond have outlined for us a clear and coming reality – many small churches in America are going to close their doors over the next 10-20 years. What is important about this book is that it offers a dignified and redemptive solution to this regrettable phenomenon. Too many churches are like people who go into denial about their impending death, and waste and loss is virtually always the result. Gray and Dumond provide a reasonable plan to transfer assets to the next generation – from death to life. Sounds rather Christ-like, does it not?
— Rev. Byron Beck, Senior Pastor of Fellowship General Baptist Church, Poplar Bluff, MO.

TABLE OF CONTENTS

FOREWORD

By Gary L. McIntosh

Aging has a way of making us look at life from a different perspective than when we were younger. Like many people, in the first half of my life I was concerned about making a living and being successful in my chosen profession. In the second half of my life, however, my thoughts are focused on being significant to others, particularly my own family. In short I am concerned about leaving a legacy to my children and grandchildren. I want my family to remember me as a person who loves God, loves his family, and loves others.

As the authors point out in *Legacy Churches*, a similar cycle takes place in churches (or it should). During the first years of a local congregation's life cycle an emphasis is placed on winning people to Christ, growing the worship attendance, and building a stable ministry program. Unfortunately, after a church becomes stable, it tends to travel a predicable life cycle that leads naturally to decline and closure. While a few churches are able to avert this natural cycle, eighty-five percent of churches will eventually close. None of us, of course, likes to think about a church closing. Yet, between 4,000 and 8,000 churches do so every year in North America. These churches must look at their life from a different perspective. They must decide how to leave a lasting legacy!

Stephen Gray and Franklin Dumond provide a seasoned, practical, and biblical approach that all churches can follow to leave a lasting legacy for generations to come. I am in one hundred percent agreement with them that the best way for a declining church to leave a legacy is to fund the starting of new congregations. By assisting in the birth of daughter congregations, an older church leaves a legacy that will live on in the lives of countless individuals and families for eternity. I encourage you to read this book, and then apply its insights. Generations of new believers will be glad you did.

Gary L. McIntosh, D.Min., Ph.D.
Temecula, California
September 2008

ABOUT THE AUTHORS

Stephen Gray is a Senior Consultant with New Church Specialties, a company that trains coaches and assists pastors world-wide to Start, ReStart and ReFocus their churches. He is currently serving as the Director of National Missions for the General Association of General Baptists, leading a church planting movement throughout the United States. During his twenty-one year ministry, Gray has planted churches in Nebraska and Missouri, and has transitioned churches in Illinois, Kansas and Nebraska.

Gray is the author of three books: *Full Disclosure: The F-Words of Church Planting* (2008), *Planting Fast-Growing Churches* (2007), *Recommissioned: A Fresh Look At Church Planting* (2006), as well as two church planting manuals: *A Comprehensive Manual for Church Planting* (2006), and *How To Organize And Register A New Church (2006).*

Gray earned both his Master of Divinity and Doctor of Ministry from Asbury Theological Seminary. He and his wife Marlene have three daughters and one grandson.

As a church pastor for more than 30 years **Dr. Dumond** served in rural, urban and county seat locations. After sixteen years in his last pastorate, Dr. Dumond began serving in a denominational role in 2005 as Director of Congregational Ministries for the General Association of General Baptists. In this role he directs ReFocus training for pastors and church leaders, consults with churches regarding local church health, and coordinates other training needs for local churches. He also serves as a Senior Consultant with New Church Specialties.

While teaching at Southeastern Illinois College he authored study guides and practice exams for *Coon's Psychology: A Modular Approach to Mind and Behavior (10th Edition)*. In his denomination he has authored *Pastor Compensation Guide (2005, 2006)* and *Pastor Search Handbook (2006).*

Dumond earned his Master of Divinity at Southern Seminary, and his Doctor of Ministry at Oakland City University.

He and his wife Winda have three sons.

ACKNOWLEDGEMENTS

It is with a great deal of joy that I thank Jesus, my guide, my life, my hope, and my Savior for the opportunity to serve Him these many years. I fully and wholeheartedly acknowledge that He is the only reason I am able to accomplish anything significant. I pray that He will afford me many more years.

I also want to thank my wife and children for their persistent love and support. God has truly blessed me with a strong family. Many hours have been spent working on this project and they have been gracious enough to allow me the opportunity to finish the work.

Finally I want to thank my denominational family, the General Association of General Baptists, for granting me the privilege of serving them as their National Missions Director.

Stephen Gray

All of us are products of the unique background and life experiences that the Lord uses to mold and shape us. I remain continually indebted to those teachers, preachers, and youth workers who took a little time with one young boy growing up in Oklahoma. Those life lessons of discipleship, love for the Lord Jesus, and devotion to His church have guided me across the years.

All of us are also products of those people we have brought into our lives. My wife, my sons, and those young men I have mentored have each helped shape my faith and my understanding.

Finally all of us are also the products of those people who have allowed us to minister and serve. I remain thankful that a few churches and a denominational staff have trusted me enough to allow me the privilege of ministry.

Franklin Dumond

INTRODUCTION

Tough Times

Sometimes life is just plain tough. It would be nice if we could escape the tough times, hide from them, or ignore their existence, but we can't. Life happens and circumstances arise that are hard to deal with. We may try to avoid these tough times only to realize there are no detours or shortcuts. While the power of positive thinking may help us cope, it does not make tough times easier. The proverbial "silver-lining" cliché doesn't make tough times easier either. Tough times are exactly that, tough.

During these difficult times, we try to find ways to comfort ourselves. For those of us who know Christ, it is God's word that calms our hearts and minds. Yet, while His word may calm our spirit, it doesn't exempt us from the difficult emotional journey.

These tough times come from multiple directions. Sometimes innocent, well-meaning people make destructive choices that end up causing us pain. We unintentionally get caught in their wake, trapped in their mud, or pulled into the consequences of their poor decisions. Other times we discover that a tough time was cast upon us intentionally. In both cases it's easy to feel like a victim.

In reality, some of the toughest things we deal with in our lives are a result of our own poor choices. Everyone, from time to time, makes foolish and sinful choices and inevitably experiences the consequences of those bad decisions. Paul wrote, "Do not be deceived: God cannot be mocked. A man reaps what he sows." (Gal. 6:7). We may wish it wasn't always true, but we do reap what we sow.

Still, some of life's toughest times can't be traced to our behavior or anybody else's for that matter. Life happens, and all we can do is nod our head and realize that these times are a result of the fall of mankind. Paul shared with the believers in Rome, "The creation waits in eager expectation for the sons of God to be revealed. For the creation was subjected to frustration, not by its own choice, but by the will of the one who subjected it, in hope that the creation itself will be liberated from its bondage to decay and brought into the glorious freedom of the children of God" (Rom 8:19-21). Because of the fall, we are destined to experience hardship. It is the price we pay for living on a fallen planet.

So, how do we handle these tough times in our lives? As human beings, all of us react differently when tough times come our way. Some try to ignore it, others fall apart, and still others, especially those in the church world, tend to super-spiritualize these events and fall into what we call the "Pollyanna Syndrome". *Pollyanna*, a Disney movie, was released in 1960. It is a wonderful movie about a little girl's quest to show a town how the power of a positive attitude can overcome any difficulty.

After the death of her missionary parents Pollyanna is sent to live with her rich aunt in a small town called Harrington. Pollyanna quickly discovers that her aunt is a mean-spirited, controlling person who casts a shadow over the whole town. Because of her aunt everyone in Harrington is bitter, sad, and frustrated. So, Pollyanna makes it her life's goal to change the town's attitude through kindness and the power of positive thinking. Pollyanna teaches people to think positively in every situation. Why? Because she believes that if they change their attitudes about life, and the tough times they face, everything will work out okay.

Later, however, Pollyanna loses that innocent spirit when she falls out of a tree and is severely injured. But don't be alarmed; as with every good Disney movie, Pollyanna's happy spirit returns and the story ends with a positive outlook on one of life's most difficult times.

This story is powerful and heart-warming. But let's be real. No matter how hard we try, no amount of "Pollyanna thinking," will make our tough times better. In fact, when these tough times come, they usually make no sense. We spend day after day trying to understand why we are going through this and what the future will hold for us, but to no avail. It may take years before we even begin to understand the value of these tough times. The truth is that we live in a tough world where tough things happen all the time.

Maybe you are reading this book because you're going through one of those tough times. Namely, the church you love and have worshiped in for years has been slowly losing its effectiveness in the community. After many years of service, sacrificial ministry, and lives impacted, the end seems to be lurking just outside the doors. The once lively and vibrant building you call your church home seems more like a museum. Your church may even be wrestling with the idea of closing its doors. What are you to do? Where do you go for answers? Is there a bright side to this tough time? That is what we hope to help you discover as you read this book.

CHAPTER ONE

Lessons from the life of Joshua

Joshua was a man caught in the middle of an extremely tough time. Moses, long time leader of the Israelites, was dead, and Joshua was left holding the bag. Put yourself in his position for just a moment. He had thousands of people depending on him for their future and he was probably anxious about, if not actually frightened by, the daunting task.

To make matters worse, God spoke to Joshua in the midst of his fear. His words weren't very comforting, at least to begin with. God said, "Moses my servant is dead. Now then, you and all these people, get ready to cross the Jordan River into the land I am about to give to them—to the Israelites" (Josh.1:2). Ouch!

The Israelites had loved and followed Moses for over 40 years. He was the only leader they had known. Now he was dead and Joshua was being called to fill his shoes. God says, "Moses is dead." God pulls no punches. He doesn't water down the facts. He doesn't use phrases like "Moses has passed on, kicked the bucket, fallen asleep, or passed away." The brutal reality was that Moses was dead and Joshua was in a tough spot.

Why was God so brutally frank? Why didn't God just step in and perform a miracle by raising Moses from the dead? After all, God knew the importance of Moses' leadership. He knew how the people loved and respected Moses. If He wanted to, God could have raised Moses back to life. Nothing is beyond His ability! Yet, God didn't raise Moses from the dead. God's brutal statement of the facts was a proclamation of the end of an era. Let that sink in for a moment. How would you have responded?

Could it be that God wanted Joshua to deal with the reality of this tough time? Moses was dead and there was no getting around it; there was no way to soften the blow or cure the insecurities within the people's hearts. The whole nation was at a crossroads. They were scared and concerned about their future, and now Joshua, a good soldier but an untested executive leader, was in charge.

God, however, continues to speak to Joshua even in the midst of his fear and insecurity. The lessons God teaches Joshua, through this experience, can help you make sense of your tough times as well. If you are part of a congregation reading this book because you find yourself between a rock and a hard place, consider the lessons of Joshua as you make decisions about the future of your church.

Can you face the brutal facts about the condition of your church? If tough decisions have to be made, can you celebrate and mourn at the same time? Does the end of an era mean the end of God's promises? Here is what we believe God shared with Joshua about his tough time. We think they can very easily apply to you as well.

First: Don't look back.

Look at Joshua 1:2. God effectively said to Joshua, "Moses is dead. Now move on!" What a hard thing to do. Our tendency as human beings is to look back. In fact, the older you get the more you tend to reflect on what once was. Your hair was longer and thicker. Your muscle tone was better. Your body used to function the way God intended. Your teeth used to be a permanent part of your body. We call those days the "good old days." No matter where you live, if you get into a crowd of older adults you will hear about physical ailments and be regaled with stories of yesteryear.

Congregations do the same thing, don't they? Countless hours are spent looking back at the "good old days," hoping they will soon return. Like mythical stories of powerful Viking leaders, parishioners share story after story of how the church use to be filled with laughter, singing and life. If only things could return to the way they were, then everything would be better. Leaders lament over the church they once knew and loved, but the Pollyanna syndrome keeps them from facing reality.

In essence God said to Joshua, “Don’t live in the past. Prepare for the future. Move on.” Those words apply to the church as well. The tendency of the Israelites was to look back at the way things had been. Numerous times the Scripture tells us how the people of Israel wished they were back in Egypt. That is hard to imagine. The Israelites had seen the power of God, experienced His presence like never before, and lived off of the goodness of His provision. Yet they were willing to trade a future in the Promised Land for a life of slavery. God wanted them to look forward, not back.

That doesn’t mean the past is always to be considered bad. As the Israelites crossed over the Jordan, Joshua chose twelve men, one from each tribe, to gather twelve stones from the river and build an altar of remembrance. Why? They were to be a sign of God’s past goodness and a promise of future blessing. The altar was to serve as a sign to future generations (Josh. 4:6).

If you read Joshua 4:6 in its context you will discover that God didn’t tell the Israelites to build the altar so they could idolize it, long for it, or mourn over it. God did not intend for them sit around this alter and say, “If only things were today like they were yesterday. If only we could have the glory of the former days.” The altar was more than just a reminder of the past. It also stood as a promise of God’s continued goodness. In essence, they could look at the altar and know that God is unchanging even in the midst of constant change. He is the same “yesterday and today and forever” (Heb. 13:8).

When God told Joshua, “Moses is dead,” He was not telling Joshua that Moses didn’t matter. God was not trying to downplay, make light of or make insignificant the past leadership of Moses. Instead, God needed Joshua to push forward because there was a lot of work to be done and an unhealthy focus on the past would not serve His purposes.

Nothing has changed in the last few thousand years. God still reminds us today that history is to be lived out, not lived in. History is a great teacher but a cruel master. Unfortunately far too many seek to live in the past. The desire to return to a period of growth and glory is strong in many congregations. The altar has been built and members sit around and idolize what once was.

Think about your church and all the marvelous things God has accomplished over the years. How many people have found a relationship with Christ because of your faithfulness? How many lives have been touched because your ministry trained new, young leaders? How has the community been served in the name of Jesus? The past should be considered a blessing and celebrated, but not lived in.

Many years after the Israelites crossed the Jordan, Solomon built a beautiful temple in Jerusalem. It didn't last long. In a few short years, relatively speaking, a conquering army entered Jerusalem, destroyed the temple, and dragged off many Israelites into captivity. Years later, a remnant of Israelites returned to Jerusalem and began the process of rebuilding their lives, their city, and their temple.

Ezra tells us that after the temple foundation was laid the people threw a celebratory party where a strange thing happened. While the older Israelites, who knew of the glory of Solomon's temple, wept bitterly, the younger crowd rejoiced. It must have been a confusing sight. Why was the older group mourning? Because they knew of the greatness of Solomon's temple and they believed this new temple would never reach Solomon's standard. This group had become so focused on the past that their faith in the power of God and His ability to affect the future in a new way was shaken.

God responded to the people of Israel through Haggai. He said, "Who of you is left who saw this house in its former glory? How does it look to you now? Does it not seem to you like nothing? The glory of this present house will be greater than the glory of the former house, says the LORD Almighty" (Hag. 2:3, 9). God clearly addressed the problem. Could it be any more obvious? The Israelites desire to relive the past limited their perception of God's ability to work in the present. In essence God said to the Israelites, "Don't look back at the way things were, but look forward to see what I will do."

Second: God's plan is still in play.

When tough times hit, often we buy into the idea that everything is lost; we panic as if somehow the frustrating events of the present nullify the ministry of the past. When we are forced to think about the closing of an era we begin to ask questions like: Did we do something wrong? Was our faith not strong enough? Can we experience revival in order to get back to the way things were? It may be that in the midst of this tough time we start to play the blame game. We may say things like, "This is the way things will be when the end is near!" "Everything we have worked so hard for as a congregation to accomplish, everything we have sweated and cried over is gone." Consider this: Was God's plan for the Israelites completed once Moses died? Or, was it just a new beginning?

Can you hear the people?

"Moses was our leader," a man shouts.

"He brought us out of Egypt!" another proclaims.

"He brought down the plagues, gave us manna and water, saved us from the serpents, talked with God on the mountain, and gave us the Law," still others say.

"Now what?" a priest screams.

It would not be a stretch of the imagination to believe Joshua was caught up in those thoughts himself. It is, after all, part of our fallen human nature to think pessimistically when tough times hit. Churches often experience this kind of thinking when a beloved pastor leaves. He was their leader and now that he is gone, what will they do?

But God said to Joshua, "I will give you every place where you set your foot, as I promised Moses" (Josh. 1:3). Joshua knew the prophecy given to Moses. He knew God's plan. So, why did God have to tell him? Because Joshua needed to be reassured. God's plan was still in full force for the Israelites. We too sometimes need to be reminded that even when tough times hit, God is still God. His plan is not hindered by things we might consider earth-shattering.

In this new era of God's master plan, he needed fresh leadership. He needed Joshua for the job because that is who the job required in this stage. God's plan was still moving forward, even though it did not involve Moses. Was Moses' work important? Yes! Moses laid the foundation for what Joshua would now complete. Moses' work made the victories Israel would experience possible. Consider this: Could it be that God accomplished everything He intended through Moses? Is it possible that Moses had fulfilled God's intended purposes for his life?

As with Moses, could it be that God has accomplished everything He intended through your ministry and now He is calling others to complete what you began? Could prolonging something God did not intend be hindering His purposes for the future? Could it be that your work, as a church, was simply to lay a foundation others would build upon? These are difficult questions that deserve honest answers.

Remember, churches were not meant to last forever. While every local church came into existence to do God's will and take part in His master plan, closing the doors does not stop the plan of God. If closing the doors of a church is the hallmark of failure, then the Church has been failing for thousands of years. Think about the churches of Acts. Were these churches insignificant because they don't exist today? On the contrary, without their hard work, determination, sacrifice, and love you may not have had the opportunity to experience Christ as your Lord and Savior. Every local church today can trace its lineage back to the churches of Acts. We are their legacy. Had they not given their all, put it all on the line, you may not have had the joy of worshiping in the local church you call home.

Be assured, God's plan moves forward in spite of the apparent problems in a church. Even if a church decides to close its doors, the Kingdom of God will not be halted. We see so dimly the things of God, but He sees the big picture. His glorious plan marches on!

Third: God never promised a bed of roses.

God reminded Joshua four times to be strong and courageous. Why did God repeat it so many times and what might that imply about Joshua? Could it be that Joshua was afraid, that he knew tough times were ahead? God was reassuring Joshua to calm his spirit.

We need to be reminded in the same way. God's work is hard! You cannot escape the fact that God has called us to serve Him in the midst of a world that hates Him. God needs us to have enough courage to be involved in His work and to do His will.

Sometimes we get the wrong impression about what it means to be in the center of God's will. We think it should be easy and that we should never suffer any difficulties, hardships, brokenness, or failures. Have you ever heard someone say, "If we as a church are in the center of God's will everything will go well for us, everything will be all right. To be in the center of God's will is the safest place on earth"? Is that true? Think through church history: opposition, persecution, martyrdom. When was being in the center of God's will ever the safest place on earth?

Jesus told his disciples, "If anyone would come after me, he must deny himself and take up his cross and follow me" (Matt. 16:24). That was not a call to safety, but a call to self-denial. In Christ's day the cross was not a clean, shiny symbol worn around the neck. It was an instrument of shame and death. Think about this: Jesus was in the center of the Father's will and it cost him his life. The disciples were in the center of the will of Christ and all but one suffered martyrdom.

History is replete with stories of thousands upon thousands of Christ-followers who have been beaten, and slaughtered for the sake of Christ. You see, the center of God's will is not the safest place; rather, it's the most dangerous and yet most rewarding place you will ever live. James wrote "Count it all joy, my brothers, when you meet trials of various kinds" (James 1:2). James knew that as Christ-followers it's not a matter of if, but when.

So keep a proper perspective. There will be trials, but God is trustworthy and will fulfill His promises.

Joshua's Response

So, how did Joshua respond to God's instructions?

> So Joshua ordered the officers of the people: "Go through the camp and tell the people, get your supplies ready. Three days from now you will cross the Jordan here to go in and take possession of the land the Lord your God is giving you for your own" (Josh 1:10-11)

Joshua responded with a step of faith in full obedience. Did Joshua have full understanding of what he was doing? Doubtful! Did Joshua have full assurance in himself? Doubtful! Did he believe it was going to be easy? Doubtful! Joshua understood tough things are tough. So why did he move forward so quickly? Because Joshua had an unshakable faith in God's power and promises. Joshua knew God had a plan.

At the end of his life, Joshua reminded the people once more, "You know with all your heart and soul that not one of all the good promises the Lord your God gave you has failed. Every promise has been fulfilled; not one has failed." (Josh. 23:14)

Tough times are tough. In the life of a church no issue can be tougher than considering the end of an era. Will this experience be easy? No! Will you have full understanding of why you are in this position now? Probably not, but don't look back!

Celebrate what God has done through your ministry and realize that God's plan is still moving on even when it seems lost.

Pick the Fruit

A pastor once told a story about a beautiful plum tree that stood in an old farmer's yard. This tree had provided fruit to the community for over twenty years. The old farmer loved his tree. It was his pride and joy. One day a violent storm swept across the community, hit the old farmer's land, and twisted the prize plum tree from its roots, leaving it lifeless.

After the storm had blown over, the neighbors began venturing out of their homes to survey the damage. A few of the neighborhood men gathered in the old farmer's yard and stood in a silent circle, gazing down at that once-beautiful plum tree, now ruined beyond repair. Finally, one of the men asked, "What are you going to do with that tree?" After a long pause, the old farmer replied, "I'm going to pick the fruit and burn the rest."

What a great lesson for us when we are facing tough times. We too can "pick the fruit and burn the rest." We can gather all the good from a sad event and get on with life. We can take from this hard experience everything we have learned and celebrate the goodness of God. We can take something positive from a dreadful disappointment and praise God for His faithfulness, insights, and blessings.

If you're reading this book and your church is at the threshold of closure, you are not alone. Hundreds of churches across the Unites States face this tough dilemma every year. Keep in mind that the decision to close a church does not need to be considered a negative, faithless act. Your local church played a significant part in God's Kingdom work.

This tough time can be faced in one of two ways. We can pick the fruit, keep the seeds found within as a reminder of what once was, clutch them in our hands never let go. Or, we can pick the fruit, savor its juices, and plant the seeds found within. We can keep the seed and agonize over the tree's demise, or we can trust that God has a plan. The choice is ours.

Jesus told the crowds around him, "I tell you the truth, unless a kernel of wheat falls to the ground and dies, it remains only a single seed. But if it dies, it produces many seeds" (John 12:24). Every piece of fruit has a seed. That seed can be used to produce another glorious fruit tree, if it is planted. God can use the seed found within a closing church to produce more fruit and enable your church to leave an eternal legacy.

CHAPTER TWO

Leaving A Legacy

In 1987 John Wimber, one of the founding leaders of the Vineyard movement, wrote a story about a mission-minded church in New York City that closed its doors after years of faithful service to God.[1] While he never revealed the name of this church, his story is one worth sharing.

The final act of this dying church was to hold a funeral service in order to celebrate its life and ministry in the community. What happened at this service was nothing short of remarkable. Wimber didn't stay for the whole service, but later received word that over twenty thousand people, representing fifty-six different churches, came to celebrate the death of this church. What makes this so remarkable is the fact that every person who came to worship throughout the day had been part of a new work started through the faithfulness of this aged and dying church.

All day long pastors and lay leaders came forward to praise God for the church's vision, generosity, and support. One particular individual came forward and shared how this dying church unselfishly gave to the very end. In one final, great act of love, this church gave away all of its best leaders and givers in order to help plant eleven new churches over the course of a year. That act of selfless giving ultimately led to the death of the church. But, what a legacy!

---

1. John Wimber, "Sent into the Harvest Field," Equipping the Saints (volume 1, number 5, September/October 1987), pages 2-4.

Although the pulpit is now empty, the organ is silent, and the playful laughter of little children no longer rings through the halls, it is impossible to quantify the impact this church will have on future generations of Christ-followers. The doors may be closed, but the ministry of this church has picked up speed. Even in closure, this church's vision and ministry will live on through the ministry of its children. Because the leaders of this church made a commitment to give birth to new churches, its ministry will never be silenced; its legacy lives on! This example teaches us that death does not need to be the final act. Maybe someday you will be able to share your own stories of new life from the ashes of death.

From Florida to California, Maine to Washington, churches are beginning to catch the vision of leaving a legacy through giving birth to another church. Like the proverbial Phoenix rising from the ashes, the vision and ministry of a closing church is finding new meaning and life through their investment in a new church. As a final act of love, the church is laying down its life for others.

It may seem a little odd to tackle such a difficult subject. However, we hope that by the end of this book you've changed your mind and learned to appropriately celebrate and appreciate the death of a church.

The State of the Church

Over the last few years, researchers like Gallup, The Barna Group, and the Association of Religious Data Archives have attempted to get a clear picture of the state of the church in America. Until recently, it was widely accepted that over 40 percent of Americans attend church on a regular basis.[2] If these numbers are right then over 130 million Americans fill our churches on any given Sunday. That's not a bad figure, but are these numbers accurate? Are we really doing that well? New research has revealed this statistic of 40 percent to be overstated and misleading.

In 2004 David Olson, director of the American Church Research Project, shattered the popular belief that almost half of Americans go to church. Olson discovered that overall church attendance in the U.S. was actually around 17.5 percent. If Olson's numbers hold true, the church is at a historic low and in danger of losing any significant influence on the American culture.

2. http://www.barna.org/FlexPage.aspx?Page=BarnaUpdate&BarnaUpdateID=135.

Why does such a large gap exist between the former popular belief and Olson's research? The answer lies in the way Olson gathered his data. Prior to Olson's research, individuals were asked about their habits concerning church attendance. Olson took a different approach by studying the actual attendance records of churches across the nation. He discovered that far fewer Americans attended church than what was previously believed.

The gap between these two percentages has been attributed to a sociological phenomenon called the Halo Effect.[3] Simply put, the Halo Effect is a fancy way of saying the people gave the answers they thought would make them look good, at the expense of being truthful. Human beings have been trying to make themselves look better than they really are ever since sin entered the world. That shouldn't be a surprise to us. The Halo Effect is just another term for this age-old problem. For example, in most post-election polls a wide gap almost always exists between people who claim to have voted and those who actually voted.

Another alarming fact has to do with the rate of population growth versus church growth. In 2007 the American population climbed to over 300 million.[4] However the attendance averages within most American churches has remained unchanged for well over a decade. In 1990, approximately 52 million Americans attended worship each week. Fifteen years later, in 2005, the number remained relatively unchanged. While the United States population continued to explode from 1990 to 2005, the average worship attendance, as a percentage of the population, declined almost 3 percent.[5]

What does that tell us? The church is not keeping up with current population growth trends within the United States. According to Olson's research, if the trend continues, by 2020 the percentage of Americans attending worship could drop from 17.5 percent to 14.7 percent.[6] Stop right now and just let that percentage sweep over you. If that doesn't cause you to gain a new sense of urgency, check your pulse and make sure your heart is still beating. Even if every church in America begins to grow considerably, to keep up with the population growth, we will have to plant many, many more churches. It is simply a matter of survival.

---

3. David T. Olson. *The American Church in Crisis: Groundbreaking Research Based on a National Database of over 200,000 Churches.* (Grand Rapids: Zondervan, 2008) page 28.
4. http://factfinder.census.gov/servlet/SAFFPopulation?_submenuId=population_0&_sse=on.
5. Olson. *The American Church in Crisis:* pages 36-37.
6. Ibid page 175.

Some may ask, “Don’t we have enough churches in America? Why can’t we just fill up these existing churches?” It is hard to estimate how many churches exist in the United States. Some estimate as low as 300,000, others have estimated as high as 450,000. Whatever that number may be, the vast majority of churches in America (roughly 80 percent) are in a state of plateau or decline. Plateaued churches show little change in average worship attendance. Declining churches show continued reductions in average worship attendance. After years of decline these churches are now experiencing a new stage in their life cycle (more on life cycles later) making it difficult to gain any positive momentum. Some of these limiting factors involve size, location, mind-set, money, leadership, age of the organization, and negative history.

One of the main factors limiting a church’s growth potential is age. Both the ages of the congregants as well as the age of the church itself play a role in its limitations. Research supports the fact that the longer a church is around and the older the average age of a congregation gets, the more it settles into a routine and loses steam. Consider this: between 2005-2006 over 57 percent of churches over 40 years of age were in a state of decline.[7] The older the church, the more difficult it becomes for a church to grow.

The difficulty for churches in this situation is the realization that few, if any, children and teens remain to sustain the church in the next generation. If you are feeling a little frustrated about what you’re reading, you are not alone. No church is exempt from this potential problem. Even well-known mega-churches throughout the Unites States are scrambling to re-engineer themselves due to the problem of an aging congregation. Even if many churches won’t admit it, they are trying desperately to correct a downward trend in attendance. Over half the churches in America will soon be facing major decisions about their future. Every local church whether large or small will, at some point, have to face the fact that it is aging.

Most large churches will not feel the impact of an aging congregation as readily, but smaller churches will experience the effects of aging at an accelerated pace. Unlike medium and larger sized churches, the smaller church experiences this dilemma with a greater sense of urgency. Why? Because the smaller church has limited people and resources from which to draw. It’s a vicious cycle! As the church ages it struggles to stay alive

7. Ibid page 84.

and often pours most of its limited energy and resources into a fight for survival. As this happens, the church loses its sense of vision and mission. The church's mission turns inward, shifting from reaching the lost to staying alive. The more inwardly focused the church becomes, the more disconnected they are from the outside world. The more disconnected a church becomes, the less influence and impact they have on the community. The less impact and influence a church has on the community, the more rapidly attendance declines. The more attendance declines, the more limited resources become.

We are not implying that smaller, struggling churches, which dominate the American religious landscape, have no value. The smaller church, without a doubt, has been a major player in the formation of religious culture in America. In fact, most churches in America are relatively small. The average church in America has "seventy-five people in regular attendance,"[8] with an average attendee's age around fifty-five. Over 50 percent of all churches in America have fewer than one hundred attendees, and 35 percent have fewer than fifty-five regular attendees.[9] These smaller congregations have, in no small way, kept the American church afloat. So, the issue is not necessarily size. The main issue that will determine a church's viability is whether or not it can engage the culture through the ability to contextualize and make meaningful the Gospel of Jesus Christ. But let's be honest, it takes money and people to do ministry in this culture. Yet, many churches across our land are using every available resource just to keep the doors open.

What are we really trying to say? Imagine what might happen if the energy and resources used by these churches in the final stages of their life cycle were poured into starting a new, vibrant church. It is a widely accepted fact that it is significantly easier, and more cost effective, to start a new congregation than it is to revitalize or restart an older, dying congregation. This is not an attempt to downplay the power of God or His ability to move in a powerful way. Nothing is impossible with God! We are, however, reinforcing the understanding that death is a natural part of life. The human body is our proof. From the moment we are born, we are on a journey toward death. Our bodies are held captive by this life cycle. Death is an inescapable reality. Death is not something to

8. Scott Thumma and Dave Travis, *Beyond Megachurch Myths: What We Can Learn from America's Largest Churches*. (San Francisco: Jossey-Bass, 2007) page 45.
9. Gary L. McIntosh ,. *One Size Doesn't Fit All: Bringing Out the Best in Any Size Church*. (Revell. Grand Rapids, MI. 1999) page 17.

fear, rather something to celebrate and for which we should all prepare. For the Christ-follower, death is just the beginning of something greater. The local church is really no different. Every church has a life-duty to perform and a life cycle to follow. If done properly, your church's ministry and legacy can live on beyond your wildest dreams.

As stated earlier, if you find yourself in this frustrating and depressing state, you are not alone. Almost every local church, district, association, and denomination is struggling with the effects of decline. In a recent post on churchcentral.com, Ken Walker reported that the Southern Baptist Convention, one of the largest church families in the world, is on course to close 50 percent of its churches by the year 2030. In our own denominational family, General Association of General Baptists, we also have the potential to experience the same percent of closure.

In a state of panic, many churches do everything within their power to keep their doors open. No expense is spared in propping up a desperate situation. While that solution may have positive short-term returns, these frantic efforts usually only delay the inevitable.

There is no doubt the church in America is experiencing a crisis. We really have only two choices in the midst of this crisis: panic or plan. The crisis we face as a church can be viewed as a sign of the times, or as an opportunity to reengage the culture through the strategic, purposeful planting of new churches. It could be that we do a little of both by allowing our panic to force us to make good plans. We are at a crossroads over the next decade that could propel us into the future with greater effectiveness or cause us to fade away with nothing more than a quiet little whimper. The choice is ours, but we must make the choice with a great sense of urgency. As aging churches begin to close their doors, financial giving decreases, which in turn makes less money available to utilize in the starting of new churches. What's the answer? We must help local churches develop a proper theology of death, convince them to give up on a nominal life support existence and enable them to leave a legacy.

CHAPTER THREE

A Proper Theology of Death

Since death is an inevitable fact of life, how is the Christ-follower to view death? What is a proper theology of death? The Apostle Paul believed God was able "to do immeasurably more than all we ask or imagine, according to his [Christ's] power that is at work within us" (Eph. 3:20). Did that refer to life on earth or life beyond the grave? The answer is simple: both! God's power not only gives us life abundantly, but also life eternally. For the Christ-follower, death is not the end; rather, it is just the beginning of something greater. Paul summarized it best: "For me to live is Christ, to die is gain" (Phil. 1:21). To die, at least for the Christian, is the great adventure all of us wait to experience. The writer of Hebrews penned, "It is appointed for all men to die once" (Heb. 9:27). No one can escape death. It is the great equalizer of all men. And yet, everyone seeks to avoid it.

We live in a culture that promotes a never-ending search for the Fountain of Youth. Thousands of Americans stream to the doctor each year for botox injections, face-lifts and tummy tucks, in hopes of beating the odds of aging. Death is viewed, by this culture, as the enemy rather than a glorious end and a new beginning. Unfortunately, this secular view of death has permeated the theology of the Church. Too many congregations have bought into the idea that "survival at any cost" is the only faithful road to travel. Has the Church lost a meaningful theology of death? The scriptures remind us time and again that for the Christ-follower death will lead to new life. It shouldn't be odd, therefore, for the Christian to celebrate and appreciate death.

If you really stop to think about it, you may come to the conclusion that sometimes more can be accomplished through death than through continued existence. No one understood this better than Jesus. Through His death, resurrection, and ascension, the Holy Spirit came to live in and empower us. Jesus told His disciples, "I tell you the truth: It is for your good that I am going away. Unless I go away, the Counselor will not come to you; but if I go, I will send him to you" (John 16:7). Earlier in Jesus' discussion about His impending death He told His disciples, "Unless a kernel of wheat falls to the ground and dies, it remains only a single seed. But if it dies, it produces many seeds" (John 12:24). Once again Jesus taught that his death would bring about fruit in ways His continued earthly ministry would not.

A few chapters later, Jesus drove the point home. "I tell you the truth, anyone who has faith in me will do what I have been doing. He will do even greater things than these because I am going to the Father" (John 14:12). Jesus did not see His own death as a failure. It seems fanciful to believe that we could do greater things than the Savior, but through His death, and the subsequent sending of the Spirit, the Kingdom of God was propelled across the world. Through the power of the Holy Spirit, we are empowered, gifted, called, and sent on a co-mission with Jesus.

Likewise, the death of a church does not need to be seen as an end or a failure. Local churches plateau, decline, and die. That's a fact! David Olson estimated that over 32,000 churches closed their doors in the last decade.[10] Let's break that number down: in the last ten years, 3,200 churches closed every year, 267 closed every month, 62 closed every week, and 9 closed every day. Frightening isn't it? And yet, it is a simple part of the life cycle.

Like people, churches live, grow, experience wonderful fulfillment, and eventually live out the fullness of their life cycle. It is a natural part of the process and one that should not be feared. Unfortunately many believers have bought into the idea that their church was meant to last until Jesus comes. That is simply not the case.

We have to be willing to accept that local churches were not intended to be eternal. Instead, we should view them as stopping-off points in the history of God's Kingdom work in the community.

---

10. Olson. The American Church in Crisis. page 120.

A Proper View of the Church

There is a big difference between the local church and the universal, eternal church (also called the body of Christ). Christ's church is eternal and will never die. It is the Bride of Christ for which He will return someday. The local church is a specific community of believers. The local church is part of the universal church, but not the whole. Those involved in these local communities will eventually and naturally age, move away, experience decline and ultimately die. This is not a new concept. Churches have always experienced this life cycle. The local community you commonly refer to as "your church" will one day experience an end. That may seem fatalistic, but we assure you it is true.

God called your church, when it was founded, into existence. God calls every community of believers into existence through His providence and sovereignty. Every local church is birthed in God's heart with a specific purpose in mind. No church comes to be through the intelligence, wit, or whim of any human being. We simply aren't smart enough to do this on our own. Therefore, we believe that God is ultimately in control of every church's destiny. Some churches last longer than others; some are here for only a short season. In that season, the sovereignty of God allows each church to accomplish great and powerful things that have eternal value. So, whether a church stays alive for a hundred years or whether it remains for only a few months, God accomplishes his intended purposes. Sermons are preached, lives are changed, and sacrifices are made for the cause of Christ. Because of this, no Bible-believing and Bible-teaching church that ends up closing its doors can be considered a failure.

It all really comes down to your understanding of the universal church and your viewpoint of how the local church fits within the greater work of Christ. "There is a spiritual legacy in every one of these churches that will never die, even if the church physically closes. The spiritual impact of that local church will live on throughout eternity."[11] Whether or not you agree with that statement will help to determine how you approach the task of leaving a legacy.

Keep this in mind: if a church closing indicates a failure, then all

---

11. Larry McKain, *Falling in Love with the Church: Building Agenda Harmony for Church Health and Church Multiplication Movements* (Kansas City, New Church Specialties,2004) page 161.

of the churches written about in Acts were miserable failures. Not one of these ancient churches exists today. What remains, however, is their legacy. The churches of Acts were springboards, stepping stones in the history of the Church. Each of these churches was uniquely called into existence for the spreading of the gospel. They served as the foundation for future works. Every church, including yours, exists today because the churches of Acts were sending bodies that did not think about self-preservation. Instead, they thought about the multiplication of the Kingdom and the spreading of the good news. That is the difference between churches with an empire mentality and churches with Kingdom mentality. Churches bent on "survival at any cost" are interested in building their own empire. Churches bent on building the Kingdom of God look beyond their own survival to the greater work of spreading the good news of Christ.

So, we've established that no local church was intended to exist forever. The problem is that many congregations see their church as a castle to protect, instead of a part of God's Kingdom-building process. We are not called to be castle fortifiers, but Kingdom builders. Instead of fighting to keep a church on life support, let's celebrate what God has done. Let's have a proper funeral and throw a party in honor of the church's faithfulness (more on this in chapter eight). It may be helpful to consider that your church is a significant part of the history of God's multiplying and spreading Kingdom.

Can you imagine what might happen if every church fighting to stay alive were celebrated, closed, and the assets used to plant another vibrant, growing church? Imagine the legacy these churches could leave for future generations?

What Now?

The unspoken desire of every church is to be a beacon of change and to leave a lasting legacy. No church, at least none of which we are aware, was ever started for the purpose of making a minimal impact on its community. Every congregation wants to leave its mark on this world, but leaving a true legacy means more than simply opening the doors on a Sunday morning. For struggling congregations in the final stages of their life cycle, the fight to stay alive is often seen as a badge of honor and an act of faithful obedience. Some may feel that allowing the doors to close will somehow reveal to the community that God is not really able to do all things. So, a strong will and an unflinching fortitude attempts to protect God from embarrassment. That noble idea actually does the very opposite, downplaying the power, sovereignty, and providence of God.

What Is A Legacy?

Legacy is a word used by many people for many different reasons. Those involved in the Green Earth Movement use the word to speak about the responsibility of leaving a clean and healthy planet for future generations. Commentators in the sports world use the word to speak of the past feats and accomplishments of star athletes. Politicians use the word to speak of historically important individuals who have changed the world through their leadership. Lawyers use the word to refer to the passing of property to a living heir. Rarely will you ever hear the word used within Christian circles in reference to a church closure.

Regardless of who uses the word, legacy always carries a connotation of a past event, which will affect, or has already affected the future. According to Webster's Dictionary a legacy is "something that is passed on from a predecessor or the past." So, to leave a legacy is to pass on to future generations something of great significance. Leaving a legacy should be the hope of every church. The simplest way for an aging church in the final stages of life to leave that legacy is through giving birth to another church. That new church can then carry your values and beliefs, continue to fulfill your missions and bring renewed life-change to a community. In a sense, you are living vicariously through the birth of a new church. Some groups have already caught the vision of leaving a legacy through church planting.

The Evangelical Covenant Church, for instance, celebrates a Legacy Church by giving a "Living Legacy Award" in the form of a baton. The baton is a symbol of the congregation's bold decision to close their doors, pass the baton, and invest in the life of a new church. This group has learned well the power of leaving a legacy. The Evangelical Covenant Church in Poway, California was such a baton-passing church. In 1995 this church closed and passed on its assets resulting in the birth of twenty-five new churches with a combined attendance of over 10,000 people! WOW!

Larry McKain, in his book *Falling In Love With The Church*, shares a powerful story of the legacy left by the Metropolitan Church, a once growing and thriving congregation in Kansas City, Missouri:

> With a congregation of well over 350, they built and paid off a sanctuary seating 400, a full-size gym and fellowship hall, a beautiful brick parsonage, all sitting on ten acres of land. Across the years, the congregation aged and began to shrink. The community changed dramatically. . . After much discussion and many weeks of prayer, a motion was unanimously proposed by the church board to the congregation:
>
> > "In order to continue to accomplish the original vision of the Metropolitan Church, we bestow our property to the Risen Lamb Church, believing that in doing so; they will carry on this great work to the glory of God".
>
> Following the church's decision to close, the Metropolitan congregation voted to give their $1,500,000 property to the Risen Lamb, a new church plant to carry on the original vision of reaching their community.[12]

The process of closing a church can be both painful and frustrating. However, we ask that you keep an open mind and a prayerful heart. We pray that you will thoughtfully consider the original intention of your church's founding families and maintain a strong sense of integrity toward their ideals and investments. Those who founded your church had a dream of reaching unsaved people. That dream does not have to end when the church doors close. The original intention of your founders was an investment in, belief in, and love for spreading the Kingdom of God. You can honor that intention and maintain the integrity of the original mission of your founders by becoming a Legacy Church.

12. McKain, Falling in Love with the Church, page 165

CHAPTER FOUR

Are There Any Alternatives?

To many believers, the thought of closing a church seems horrendous. It may even sound like a cowardly and faithless act. After all, our God can do anything! Surely there are alternatives, right?

Without a doubt our God is a great and mighty God! If He chooses, He can raise a dead church much like He raised Lazarus. Unfortunately, that line of reasoning often leads many congregations to believe that faith alone is the key to revitalization. If they simply have enough faith, God will move the mountain. But, as James says, "faith without deeds is dead" (James 2:26). In reality, most congregations find themselves in their present situation due to a fear of change and years of neglecting to engage their culture.

Make no mistake, God can do, and still does, miracles today. Nothing is impossible with God! In 1971, Dr. Rose Sims and her husband moved to Fayette, Missouri to teach at Central Methodist College. When they arrived, New Hope United Methodist Church was on the endangered species list and ready to close. The building was in disrepair, the members were well on in their years, and they had all but given up. A few years later, through the power of God, New Hope was a wonderful success story. It became, according to Dr. Sims, "one of the choicest rural appointments in the conference."[13] Fortunately, this is not the only story told about God's revival of a dying church. Throughout history,

13. Rose Sims,. New Life For Dying Churches: *It Can Happen Anywhere*. (Trilby, FL: New Life Inc., 1989) page 142.

God has intervened and resurrected many dying churches.

Yet, caution must be taken. Faith alone will not bring about the changes necessary to revitalize a church. Faith must be accompanied by hard work, complete openness to change (even if you don't like the idea of change), and a desire to do whatever it takes to bring the church back to life. You must believe as if it depends on God and work as if it depends on you. Even then, there is no guarantee of success. Keep in mind that faithful, believing churches, all throughout history, have closed their doors. Realistically speaking, once a church reaches the death phase of its life cycle, rarely will it experience significant growth and rebirth. But, we don't like to face that fact, so we fight the good fight and pray that our church will be the one that beats the odds.

We do the same thing when we experience a diagnosis of serious illness. When patients are diagnosed with a fatal disease, naturally they begin to ask tough questions. Is there any hope? Can I be cured? How long do I have? Likewise, congregations faced with the possibility of closing will naturally engage in this same practice. What have other congregations, in similar situations, attempted? Should we hire a new pastor? Should we build a new building? How long can we hold on to what we have? Is there a better alternative? Can a church turn around to find life and vitality again?

Our experience in working with many churches, asking these kinds of questions has led us to share with you the three avenues most churches travel in the hopes of revitalizing themselves: hiring new pastors, building new facilities, and merging with other congregations.

The question is, can these be viable alternatives to closing a church? To answer that question, we will share three stories about real congregations who tried to save their churches through these avenues. In order to protect their identity the names and locations of these churches are fictitious, but we assure you, the stories are real.

Growth by Merger: Bethlehem Baptist Church (West Falls, Kentucky)

Bethlehem Baptist was a relatively new church, started in 1998 by Rev. Joe Hall. As with every church planter, Joe had big dreams of starting a vibrant new church that would reach thousands of people with the gospel of Christ. Within days of moving his family to West Falls, Joe began the arduous process of gathering new members for his church. After six months of knocking on doors, throwing large parties in the park, and an expensive mass mailing to his community, Joe had a problem. Of the hundreds of contacts Joe made, only twelve adults had agreed to join this new adventure. Joe needed more than twelve adults and he knew it, but he pushed on, hoping God would do a miracle. That was a mistake he would soon regret.

Six months after the church was officially launched Joe realized he was in serious trouble. The twelve adults who had helped him start the church had formed a tight bond and weren't willing to let outsiders into the pack. The inevitable reality of an untimely death began to set in as Joe searched desperately for a solution. Joe was a fighter who had fallen prey to Pollyanna Syndrome, so he pushed on. He was not about to let his dream die that quickly.

A few miles down the road, Haven House, another struggling church plant, was facing the same fate. When Joe heard about their dilemma, he had an idea: "Why not merge the two smaller congregations into one?" So the next Sunday, after Joe had packed up the sound system and cleaned up his temporary meeting place in the local theater, he drove over to talk with the pastor of Haven House.

Dave, pastor of Haven House, was preparing to leave the little storefront facility where his church had been meeting when Joe caught up with him. It didn't take long for Joe to begin casting a vision of what might happen if the churches joined forces. Both men left that meeting excited about the idea and agreed to pursue the possibility of a merger. If everything worked out right, these two struggling churches of twenty-five each were about to become one church of fifty. Everything they needed to gain a renewed sense of vision and momentum was at their fingertips, so they thought.

With a combined forty-five years of pastoral experience, these pastors were savvy. Their years of experience gave them keen insight into handling this merger. The plan was a good one. They would make multiple changes in order to give this new work a fighting chance. The name of the church was changed to keep either group from claiming superiority, a neutral place to meet was found, and they even spent time rewriting the organizing documents. Joe and Dave were very careful not to allow either congregation to have a greater sense of control.

Everything seemed to be moving along famously. But all was not as it appeared. Underneath the surface a storm was brewing.

Three months into the merger squabbles began to occur between the congregations. Vision turned into venom and mission turned into a mess. Some members were able to accept and embrace the change; others felt a sense of obligation to resist it. Still others were just plain tired or mad. Instead of working through their differences, whole families walked away from the new church. After the smoke settled, this new congregation had dwindled to only twenty-five regular attendees. What started out as a promising idea, ended in frustration and left the new church in the same state as the original two.

To merge or not to merge; that is the question.

Merging is an option many declining churches consider, especially when two or more churches of the same denominational family exist in the same urban landscape. In fact, it seems to be a growing trend. Some, like United Methodists, use mergers as a denominational strategy. Yet, rarely do mergers produce the expected results. Stories do exist of powerful instances where a merger was a saving grace, but these seem to be the exceptions, not the rule. More often than not, mergers end in disaster.

The rationale for attempting a merger goes like this: *If two declining, struggling churches can merge into one larger church, we will be able to do more ministry, have more money, add on to a decaying building, and build a larger membership base.* In theory, it sounds like a good idea—in reality, it very rarely pays off. Mergers are tough. The belief that two struggling congregations will produce one strong, vibrant church borders on mythical. So, merging should be a last resort, if even that.

In most cases 2 + 2 will still equal 2. If a congregation of twenty-five merges with another of thirty, it will not produce a strong body of fifty-five. After time, history has proven that the new congregation will settle between twenty-five and thirty. "The success rate makes this a high-risk option"[14] and one that only a specialist could accomplish. So, why do these mergers so often fail?

---

14. Lyle E. Schaller, *A Mainline Turnaround: Strategies for Congregations and Denominations.* (Nashville: Abingdon , 2005) page 145.

Three reasons why mergers fail

1. Unhealthiness.

While Bethlehem Baptist Church sought to change in a positive way, the underlying issues of unhealthiness were never addressed. In fact, neither congregation stopped to consider why they were in their present situation. The potential positive change was stymied by unchanged methods, mind-sets, and traditions. No matter how much positive change a congregation makes, if it does not address the underlying issues, progress will be halted every time. As mentioned earlier, once a church reaches the point of death in its life cycle, revitalization is possible, but not very likely. Even if one church has addressed these issues, more often than not a struggling congregation attempts to merge with another church in the same state of decline that has not addressed the underlying, unhealthy issues that brought decline.

2. Vision

The power of a unifying vision cannot be overstated or underestimated. Every church has a vision of a preferred future. But often two merging congregations do not articulate or communicate their unshared and unspoken visions. Mergers muddy the waters as it concerns vision and direction. A merger will often create a new church with multiple, conflicting visions. These conflicting visions will create tension and cause an unhealthy atmosphere in the church. Factions from each existing congregation will defend their model for ministry and set the stage for destructive conflict. For instance, one church may have been founded on the concept of social reform while the other was formed on the concept of building strong family-type relationships. While both visions are good, one focuses outward while the other is more inward focused. These conflicting visions may not be evident at first, but as the church begins to move forward in ministry, they become vehicles for contention.

Even if the new congregation promotes a new vision, the old ones may linger in the hearts and minds of members. Why? Because the vision of each prospective church was probably what attracted the original members. Those who remained in each church did so because they believed in the vision and direction of the church. A merger will often give a congregation a short-lived illusion of shared vision, but in reality differing opinions still exist about the ultimate direction of the church.

Never assume that people are on board with the new direction just because they give verbal assent to the vision. Only time will tell if they are truly in agreement with, and sold out, to the new direction.

3. Control

Let's be honest: two or three families in the congregation run most small churches in America. These families have either grown up in the church or were the original families who started the church. They have invested thousands of dollars, hundreds of hours of sweat-equity, and multiple years of their lives in the church. These controlling families, regardless of how right or wrong it may be, make most of the final decisions.

The problem arises when two or more congregations attempt to merge with these types of existing power structures in place. Inevitably the power brokers from each congregation will begin to vie for power in the new church. So, you can almost count on fireworks being a part of the newly merged congregation if these strong individuals are not willing to let go of their power. Tension of this nature will not help grow a church. Newcomers will sense the tension and never come back.

To pull off a successful merger takes a special person with strong leadership skills and an ability to bring a sense of control to a potential hotbed. Rarely do mergers ever produce the desired result. Statistically speaking, they are not a good bet.

Growth by Construction: Johnson Valley Christian Church (Mt. Vernon, Tennessee)

Johnson Valley Christian Church (JVCC) was a few months away from celebrating 125 years of service. Started in 1883, this modest-sized church had been a prominent part of transforming Mt. Vernon, TN. In the early to mid 1900's JVCC was the most influential church in the county. It housed some of the wealthiest and most powerful leaders in town. If only it could return to the good old days.

By 1935 JVCC was in full swing. The congregation had grown so rapidly that they decided to build a new facility on the top of the highest hill in the city. The original building, while loved by all, had lived out its potential. The leaders of JVCC began to realize that if the church were to continue to grow a new building would have to be erected to house all the new and exciting ministries. This new building would have to be twice as big as the original. With momentum on their side JVCC began to build. In a little under a year a new building had been constructed and the first Sunday the new building was opened JVCC hosted a congregation of well over 300.

Forty years later (1975) the JVCC was slowly and steadily losing its place of prominence in the community. The decline happened so slowly that it took another ten years to notice that only 35 people, most of whom were elderly, remained faithful, consistent attendees.

In the midst of JVCC's decline, an interesting trend began to develop in Mt. Vernon. New churches were being started and seemed to be growing at a rapid pace. These new churches were building new, up-to-date facilities that seemed to be attracting hundreds of people. Naturally, the remaining members of JVCC noticed the trend and came up with the perfect plan to bring their church back from the brink of death. The remaining members believed that if they were to stay current and reach new, young families, they would have to build a new facility.

Since JVCC had been a church of such great influence in the community, many of the former members had left it large sums of money. Giving had been so good that the congregation had enough money in the bank to build a beautiful, new, debt-free building. Two years later the funds were exhausted, but the new facility was finished. They had placed every dollar they had into the possibility of a new start with a new building.

The first service in the new building (July 1987) was highly anticipated. Most of the congregation showed up hours early to make sure everything was in place for the arrival of their guests. But after months of planning, only a few dozen new faces came to celebrate the opening of the new church, for a total of sixty-five. Even with the new visitors the three-hundred-seat auditorium looked hopelessly empty.

Nonetheless the congregation was excited and felt as though they had gained some much-needed momentum. The following Sunday, spirits were high as the greeters prepared to welcome last week's visitors. Five minutes before the service started only two of the previous week's newcomers returned for worship. This trend was repeated over the following weeks. It wasn't long before anticipation and excitement turned into frustration and surrender. Six months later, bankrupt and demoralized, the congregation voted to close the church and sell the property.

If you build it, they will come!

"If you build it, they will come." That phrase was made popular in the 1989 movie *Field of Dreams.* Ray Kinsella, played by Kevin Costner, was a novice farmer who began hearing a mysterious voice telling him to construct a baseball diamond in a cornfield. Once the work was completed, ghostly players came out of the cornfield to play ball.

Prior to constructing the baseball diamond, Ray and his family were close to bankruptcy. The farm wasn't providing enough cash flow to keep the family afloat. Naturally the best thing he could do was construct a baseball diamond. Right? After all, the voice promised him if he spent his last dollar building a baseball diamond, "they" would come. Funny thing about this voice, it never clarified what "they" would do.

If we were to follow the advice of a voice in our head, "they" would either refer to large men in white coats, the local priest coming to perform an exorcism, or the bank coming to seize our property. The act of building a baseball diamond in the middle of a cornfield was sheer lunacy. Yet, once the field was built paying spectators from miles around came to watch the ghostly players play ball. In the movie, Ray's foolish act saved the farm. If only it were that easy!

Unfortunately, the fanciful promise of "growth by construction" has become the strategy of many churches across the nation. The intention is pure, but the strategy is faulty. Like JVCC, many churches have poured millions of dollars into new facilities in hopes of igniting a period of growth. After the dust settles and reality sets in, these churches realize they simply prolonged the inevitable.

Growth by construction is never a good strategy for a church in decline. When should a congregation decide to build? Volumes have been written on this subject. Here are four determining factors every church should have before they even begin to consider construction.

1. A church should be experiencing strong, steady growth in its attendance, finances and overall ministries.
2. A church must have a positive forward momentum with new or expanded ministries that will be aided by new facilities.

3. A church should be consistently (80 percent) full for Sunday services.
4. Before building a new facility and burdening a congregation with debt, a church should use multiple services to alleviate overcrowding.

If a church is meeting all four of these criteria, only then should it consider building a new facility.

As with growth by merger, growth by construction doesn't address underlying unhealthiness. A few coats of paint or a shiny new facility won't help you confront the issues that brought your church to this low point in its history. Growth by construction also uses massive amounts of resources that may be better used elsewhere. The money a declining congregation uses to build one large facility or addition could be used to start multiple, fast-growing church plants.

Growth by Pastor: New Horizon Church (Van Dyke, Michigan)

A visionary leader, John Stuart, started New Horizon in 1940 during the dark years of World War II. Pastor John's vision and leadership made him one of the most influential and powerful men in Van Dyke. Not only did he start a new congregation, but his leadership was instrumental in stabilizing a hurting community that suffered major losses during the war.

Through Pastor John's leadership, New Horizon grew to be the largest church in town. Every mover and shaker in Van Dyke attended New Horizon. Without a doubt, this church was making a huge impact on the community. Because of the driving vision and passion of Pastor John, lives were changed, marriages were restored and families found wholeness and healing. It seemed as though nothing could stop Pastor John from taking the world by storm.

However, Pastor John's vigor and passion waned as age began to take its toll on his body. Thirty-five years after New Horizon's glorious birth, pastor John retired and passed the baton to a few younger leaders. The church struggled to fill the void created by Pastor John's absence and it wasn't long before everything began to fall apart.

In order to find a solution to the problem the leaders of the church hired and fired an endless train of new pastors in hopes of finding a new, young version of Pastor John. Time and again New Horizon reached new states of decline and the deacons would come to the same faulty conclusion: "It's the pastor's fault!" Over the course of twenty-five years these deacons hired and fired over twenty pastors. Rarely was a pastor able to stay more than a year. This constant turnover of leadership took its toll on New Horizon. By 2001, this once influential church had declined to a few leading families in the community. Unfortunately, during twenty-five years of decline, never once did the congregation consider that they might have played a part in the church's decline.

The present pastor, Bill Jenkins, was just another casualty of this faulty assumption. One Sunday afternoon, the leading deacon approached Pastor Bill. "Pastor," he said, "Please don't plan the monthly deacons' meeting this evening. We have already set the agenda. We have some special matters to discuss." Not wanting to seem hurt by the request, Pastor Bill agreed. That night, just a few minutes into the meeting, the chairman of the deacons turned to the pastor and said, "We've decided to let you go. The church is declining and you're just not getting the job done." By the end of the meeting everyone had agreed that when the school year had concluded, Pastor Bill would leave.

Publicly, this process was always described as a means of finding the right leader. In reality, the process of cycling through pastors was an attempt by a handful of opinionated leaders to maintain control of the church.

If Only We Had the Right Pastor.

Maybe you've heard or lived out this story. The leaders secretly meet, the pastor is given an ultimatum, and then a new pastor is called to lead the church. For many churches this cycle is repeated every one to three years. Conventional wisdom among church leaders is, "If we can just find the right leader, then we will grow."

So, deacons, elders, and church leaders of every sort spend their time in search of the perfect pastor. Once they've found their ideal leader, they sit back and await the hordes of new people who will come to hear their new pastor. Two years later, when the church remains stagnant, the leaders bid the pastor farewell and set out in search of a new candidate. Every time a new pastor leaves, a few of the members give up on the church or follow the pastor to a new location. Time after time this scenario repeats itself until only a few members are left to hold down the fort.

With no young families left, and a sullied reputation in the community, the remaining members fade away. The only noticeable legacy of a once-thriving church is an occasional obituary in the local paper indicating that a longtime member has died.

Hire or Fire?

Good leadership is hard to find. Every church in America dreams of having a strong, visionary pastor who will lead them to the Promised Land. How do we know that? Just stop and look at how the American church idolizes pastors of large growing churches. When the church doesn't grow, church leaders experience frustration, and the only conclusion they are willing to draw is: "It's the pastor's fault!" Sometimes that conclusion is true; most of the time it's not. Growth by pastor is not a good strategy to jump-start a ministry.

Congregations adopt a growth-by-pastor strategy after seeing what amazing leadership can do for a church. Too often, churches idolize leaders like Charles Stanley, Adrian Rogers, Rick Warren, and Bill Hybels, and set out to find their own world-class leader. Without a doubt these men are exceptional individuals, but their leadership skills alone are not what grew their congregations. Each of the pastors mentioned above, without reservation, would tell you that their churches grew because church members caught, owned, and worked toward the church's vision. Why is growth-by-pastor not a good strategy?

1. Relying on one person will not grow a church.

Unfortunately, local churches have become too accustomed to relying on professional clergy. No matter how you slice it, the local church was not meant to be a one-man show. Paul reminds the church in Corinth, "The body [referring to the church] is a unit, though it is made up of many parts; and though all its parts are many, they form one body" (I Cor. 12:12). Each local church is a body made up of various parts. Each part of the body was created by God to serve a function. When the body is functioning as it should, that means everyone is working together for the good of the local ministry. When the body is not functioning as a whole, but simply relying on one part of the body, the ministry will suffer.

God never intended the pastor to be the all-in-all for a congregation. According to Ephesians 4, God has given every Christian a gift to be used for His Kingdom. Every member of the church is called to participate in and own the greater vision of God's Kingdom work.

The pastor is a part of the body, but not the whole body. His unique calling is to "equip the saints for the work of ministry" (Eph 4:12 ESV), not do the entire ministry. The saying, "United we stand, divided we fall," certainly applies to the church. When all the members of a local church are working together, they will be able to accomplish much. When they rely on one man to do it all, it is the beginning of the end.

When a church is failing and about to close, it is not just a simple matter of poor pastoral leadership. Replacing a pastor may give a church a temporary boost, but in the long run it solves very little. One person cannot single-handedly overcome years of neglect and negative momentum.

2. Growth by pastor does not address the underlying systems.

Every church functions as a collection of systems. Every system is uniquely designed for a specific outcome, for example, discipleship training, worship, evangelism, and outreach. In other words, the outcome you are experiencing as a church is due more to a dysfunctional set of systems than it is to one person. This is not always true, but in most cases, a church facing decline and death can trace its problems back to a set of poorly functioning systems, not one person.

Think about this: A patient has been dealing with chronic stomach problems for three years. Every time the patient sees the doctor, the doctor orders further testing but because the patient is stubborn, and does not want to run up a huge bill, he passes on the testing and asks the doctor to simply treat the symptoms. After years of struggling through the pain the patient agrees to testing, but it is too little to late. The doctor discovers the patient has an advanced case of stomach cancer and there is little that can be done.

Too often churches do the same thing. They treat a symptom and fail to look at the deeper problem. Many churches operating on expected loyalties and tradition fail to strategically plan for the future, wrongly assuming that the systems that helped them to thrive in the '50s will carry them through the twenty-first century. Good systems and structures are foundational to a healthy, growing church. A lack of these systems will produce an unhealthy congregation with selfish tendencies.

Conclusion

While we have covered only three alternatives, experience has taught us that these are the most popular courses of action taken by churches when they are in a fight to stay alive. The fact of the matter is every Sunday churches across the nation are fighting to stay afloat through merger, construction, or leadership. Yet thousands are still closing. In our next chapter we will help you understand that only rarely does a church in the final stages of its life cycle survive.

CHAPTER FIVE

Understanding the Life Cycle

You have heard us mention life cycles throughout the book. We believe that every living organism experiences these life cycles, even a local church. Solomon once observed that there was a time and place for everything. He said there was "a time to be born and a time to die" (Eccles.3:2). His poetic description of humanity compresses life into two events; birth and death. This observation rings as true now as it did when the words were first penned.

Developmental psychologists and casual observers alike recognize that all humans must move through a normal life-cycle that begins with conception, celebrates birth, grows and blossoms into maturity, and moves into the final physical stages of decline and death. What is true of the human body is also true of organizations. These same principles of birth, growth, development to maturity, decline, and death can also be applied to the church. In essence, to live is to die. It is both normal and natural. No one can escape it.

In the beginning.

At some point in history your church did not exist. Your church was little more than a dream. The dream, once conceived in the hearts and minds of your founders, moved from a possibility to a living, breathing reality. As the church grew, it started ministries in the community and became a vital spiritual lifeline for those who lived in the area. At some point, your founders sacrificed to build a permanent facility to accommodate their rapid growth.

Throughout the early years of life, your church probably celebrated enormous growth and experienced powerful ministry success. Thirty years later however, the ministry probably reached a peak and began to slow. After an additional two decades, the success of yesteryear is celebrated, but remains little more than a memory. Now, after a glorious run of one hundred years, the church teeters dangerously on the cliff of extinction.

That story line is very common throughout the United States. Every church will eventually travel through these natural stages of life and death. These stages are referred to as a life cycle. These life-cycle stages of organizational development are often portrayed on a standard bell curve that measures attendance over a period of time. The stages include birth, growth, maturity, plateau, decline, drop-out and death.

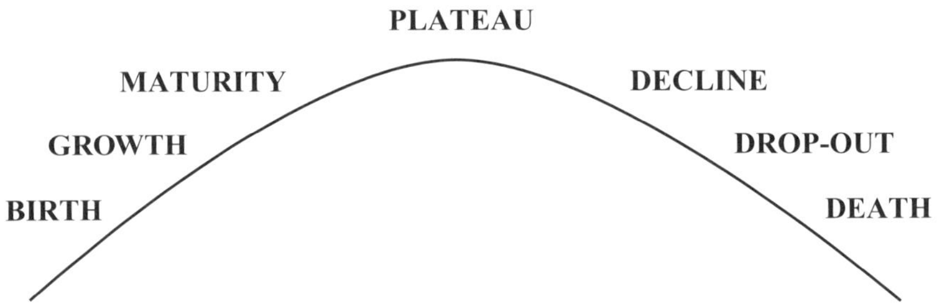

Many issues can help determine where a church finds itself on this bell curve, but most of the time the age of a church is one of the greatest determining factors. When expressed in chronological terms the life cycle may be seen in general terms of:

- Years 1-5: birth or early years of growth
- Years 6-15: maturity
- Years 15-50: plateau or refocus that leads to new birth and growth
- Years 60-80: decline and drop out if a refocus didn't take place during the period of maturity or plateau. Once a church heads down this side of the curve, it becomes increasingly difficult to regain momentum. Negative momentum is nearly impossible to stop.

- Years 80+: death or restart

Every church will move through a life cycle. From birth, the church goes through spurts of growth as it moves toward maturity. Upon reaching the stage of maturity a church will typically spend several years plateaued before beginning the journey toward decline and potential death if a successful time of refocus is not started. Some churches have been able to experience renewal and growth after years of decline, but most are gradually sliding down towards extinction.

The most vulnerable stage for a church to reach is maturity. That may seem counterintuitive, but it is in the maturity stage that churches either decide to reinvent themselves while they still have positive momentum, or protect what they have built and head down the other side of the bell curve.

While the chart shows a smooth line with natural, predictable transitions, the actual story of an organization's development is often one of stops and starts. An organization with a long history will likely have several periods of growth, maturity, plateau, and decline before another revival, rebirth of the vision, or newfound burst of energy will begin the cycle again. An organization with a long history is likely to have a much longer down-side (plateau, decline, drop-out) than it had up-side (birth, growth, maturity).

Because the life cycle is not always as predictable and smooth as many may think, it is important to avoid alarm over short periods of plateau or decline. The best possible advice for any church is to remain vigilant. Once a problem is spotted, insure that all possible measures are taken to reverse decline before it leads to drop out and death.

Life Cycle Factors

Why does a church move through these stages? What factors in the life of a church cause plateau or decline? A number of factors may influence both the speed with which a church progresses through the life cycle, and the direction a church moves in the life cycle. Some of these factors are external forces beyond the control of the congregation while other factors are internal.

1. External Factors.

The life cycle of a congregation is often influenced by factors beyond its control. Some of these external factors are community trends that impact all social organizations including churches, schools, and even local businesses. Others are external factors unique to the local church.

A) Change of landscape. A new industrial park recently expanded in a mid-town area. What had previously been a stable working-class neighborhood became a series of industrial warehouses. At first it seemed the church property would be purchased, allowing the well-established congregation the opportunity to relocate and restart. But, plans change. While the church planned to move, the planning commission drew a line on the map, saving the church property but removing the residential area from which it traditionally drew its members. The now aging congregation faces the brutal fact of rapid decline due to an external factor beyond its control. Industrialization in urban areas has, at times, eliminated entire neighborhoods.

B) Loss of population. Churches also face a downward attendance trend due to the continued decline in the population base of the entire community. The most noticeable example of this problem is seen in rural areas. Many rural towns and villages have steadily decreased in population over the last few decades as their children graduate from school, head to college and build new lives beyond the borders of their community. Years of this kind of migration have resulted in the closure of small, family-run businesses and a shortage of jobs. As the population base declines, social institutions like schools and churches suffer huge losses. Sometimes, ethnic migration diminishes a population traditionally served by a local church. Likewise, natural disasters such as hurricanes, wild fires and floods can displace the population and lead a church into decline.

C) The Triple Elder Effect. The older a church is, the more likely it is to be made up of older members. The older the members of a church, the greater will be the likelihood that the church will be served by an older pastor. When all three of these factors are combined the church may be faced with what David Olson calls the "Triple Elder Effect."[15] Once these three factors are in place, growth becomes more difficult

---

15. David T. Olson, . *The American Church in Crisis: Groundbreaking Research Based on a National Database of over 200,000 Churches* (Grand Rapids: Zondervan, 2008) page 85.

because such churches tend to resist change.

Sometimes this effect is triggered by external factors beyond the control of the congregation. For example, many counties in the United States have a higher than average median age. The national median age is around 37 years old, according to the most recent U.S. census data. Yet, in a few parts of the country the local median age is around 50-55 years. As a consequence, the aging population will have fewer young families with children. The obvious result is a hardship on local social institutions hoping to grow and maintain a meaningful existence.

As time passes and the church grows older, it may move into decline simply because of the external factor of the passage of time. Unless a local church successfully evangelizes and disciples new members, the passage of time will slowly but surely eliminate its own membership. No congregation can hold back the passage of time.

D) The rapid pace of change. In the twenty-first century, all churches are impacted either positively or negatively by the social environment's tendency toward rapid change. When VHS tapes became readily available, it seemed unlikely that they would quickly disappear after the DVD arrived. Now, the digital age rules our culture and constantly reminds us of the rapid pace of change. In a matter of a few short years we have moved from cassette tapes to compact discs to MP3 players. This rapid pace of change in our culture, and the church's failure to keep up with this rapid change, often results in the organizational life cycle being compressed into a shorter span of time.

Take, for example, the Sunny Road Baptist Church located in a very large Midwestern metropolitan area. Established in the 1950s by members who migrated from the rural southern region of the state, the church quickly grew to become a flagship church for its Midwestern based denomination. Buildings were built and ministries flourished. In the face of a major shift in the urban scene, this flagship church decided to build a large facility in the neighborhood it had served for twenty-five years. At the same time, the neighborhood went into transition due to the construction of a new interstate highway. Shortly after the building was completed, members began to migrate farther into the suburbs and soon began transferring to churches much closer to their homes.

The entire ethnic landscape of their community began to rapidly change, yet the church continued down the same ministry path. The congregation made no attempts to connect with these new ethnic groups that now populated the church's neighborhood. Decline set in. Drop-out was obvious. Death occurred about 10 years ago but the church, due to the faithfulness of a few very generous members and the rental of the unused part of their facility, has been able to stay on life support.

The inevitable took place, and now the remaining twenty-eight members have placed the building up for sale. Against the advice of denominational leaders, they are pursuing merger with another struggling congregation. This church's life cycle has been compressed to about 50 years due, in part, to the rapid pace of change in their environment.

2. Internal factors

External factors, however, are generally not the main cause of the aging and decline of a congregation. Internal factors usually have greater influence in the downward trend of a church's life cycle. For example, the arrival of a new leader may reenergize the congregation with a fresh vision. In the same way, the loss of a leader may speed the decline. Here are some of the internal factors that influence a church's life cycle.

A) Resistance to change. Change is constant in the life of a new church. Everything moves so fast and changes so rapidly that the church has to remain flexible. But once a church reaches the maturity stage of the life cycle, stability becomes the mainstay and change happens very slowly. Out of necessity, as a church matures it must become more organized. This progression, from birth to maturity, is both natural and normal. Unfortunately, this natural progression also carries with it a potential problem.

When a church is birthed, a constant flow of new attendees is the lifeblood of the church. An outward focus and strong evangelistic programs are a must if the church is to grow. Once expected growth begins, the focus of the church begins to shift in a very subtle way. New structures and programs are created to serve the faithful members. The outward focus, which built the church, begins to be supplanted by a new agenda. This new agenda is necessary, but far too often the church loses its original evangelistic drive. The congregation may still aspire to be evangelistic, but a quick look at the church's checkbook, budget, programming and calendar will give you a clear picture of the value placed on evangelism.

The real problem arises when the traditional programming of church becomes so entrenched that change is next to impossible. Resistance to change will cause the congregation to age because a purposeful and intentional attempt to engage the culture no longer exists.

In southwestern Indiana one of the earliest Baptist churches established in the first half of the nineteenth century came to be known as Bethel Primitive Baptist. The church did well for its first 100 years but did not fare too well past the middle of the twentieth century. One of the few remaining members, who maintained an affiliation with the church for nearly eighty years, observed, "Our church did well until everyone else started doing Sunday School." This blame-casting tendency kept her from seeing the real reason for her church's decline and death. Since the church resisted change and refused to adapt to a new day, all that remains of that church is a granite marker at the edge of a school parking lot.

B) Long service by same volunteers. A congregation that prides itself on long terms of service given by volunteers may unintentionally force the church into decline and drop-out. New members will leave a church out of frustration when little room is created for them to lead and to serve. Likewise, overextended members can experience burnout after serving in one area of ministry for far too long, and leave the church proclaiming that no one else cares.

C) Mismanaged conflict. Congregations that cannot handle conflict fairly, quickly, and honestly will experience a continuous pattern of division and alienation resulting in decline, drop-out and death. One great agitator of conflict in the local church is the practice of congregational voting. This practice has caused more widespread damage and ruined relationships than almost any other practice in the church.

Conflicts and disagreements over the direction of the congregation can lead to blame-casting and grudges. When these attitudes become the order of the day, a cold and unwelcoming atmosphere will permeate a church. If these attitudes are allowed to continue well beyond the actual conflict, decline and drop-out will be accelerated because the members will become so caught up in the past conflict that they cannot deal with the present.

D) Relational dysfunction. Relational dysfunction is the inability to form and maintain healthy working relationships. A church experiencing relational dysfunction will often discover its members have tied their self worth to the positions and titles they hold. A senior member of a congregation usually holds an arbitrary control over the congregation and refuses to share any responsibility. This behavior causes a rift in the church and seriously impairs personal relationships with those who resent such control. When relational dysfunction reaches this point, decline and drop-out are inevitable.

E) Debt. Debt is a funny thing. Its presence or absence may accelerate or decelerate the life cycle of a church. Debt can have a negative effect when the load reaches a critical point and every dollar a church has is used just to pay the mortgage each month. When a church is no longer able to properly fund outreach, decline and drop-out are inevitable. On the other side of the coin, the absence of debt may give a struggling congregation the ability to survive in a weakened state for a long period of time. Many declining churches have large sums of money in savings accounts. This money gives them a sense of security and ease, keeps the lights on, and provides for all their needs. It does little, however, to fulfill the Great Commission. Both scenarios are detrimental to the Kingdom.

Finding Yourself on the Life Cycle

Eighty percent of churches in the United States are either plateaued or in decline. Furthermore, many of them are able to maintain a plateaued existence for a number of years and remain blinded to the fact that they are really in a state of decline.

Is your church in a state of decline? How can you discover where your church fits in the life cycle? The four best ways to determine where your church is in the life cycle is by reviewing average annual attendance, understanding your rate of retention of first-time guests, determine the average age of regular attendees, and take a life cycle survey.

If you choose to take a hard look at your church and try to determine where it is on the life cycle bell curve, don't use membership rolls to determine the health of your church. Membership statistics will not give you a clear picture of the actual situation of a local church. Many churches have built members roles that don't reflect the true nature of their situation. In fact, many churches haven't cleaned their membership roles of absentee members and inactive members for decades.

Steps to determine your church's life cycle placement:

1. Chart your attendance records for the last three to five years. If possible use attendance records for the last ten years. What is the trend? Has attendance consistently decreased? If attendance has decreased by up to 10 percent over the last three years you are in a state of decline. If attendance has decreased more than 10 percent, you may be in a state of drop-out. If attendance has decreased over 25 percent, and a quick solution is not discovered, long term survival may be difficult.
2. If your church keeps good records on first-time guests, determine how many of these guests are returning. A church must be able to keep about 16 percent of its first-time guests to experience a growth rate of 5 percent each year. Churches that are growing rapidly keep between 25 and 30 percent of their first-time guests. Declining churches keep only about 5 to 8 percent of their first-time guests.[16] How well is your church doing at retaining first-time guests?
3. Chart the average age of your regular attendees. If the average age is over 50 and you are not experiencing at least 25 percent of your new growth through young families, you may be in a state of decline. If the average age of your regular attendees is over 65 and you are experiencing no new growth through young families, you may be in a state of drop-out. The more statistical information you are able to chart the clearer picture you get on the condition of the church.
4. Take a congregational life cycle survey. A sample of this survey can be found Appendix III.

One final question before moving on: When was the last time your church experienced a real conversion?

16. Gary L. McIntosh, *Beyond the First Visit: The Complete Guide to Connecting Guests to Your Church.* (Grand Rapids: Baker Books 2006) page 24.

The Safe Zone

Over the long haul, every organization will move through periods of growth, plateau and decline. Because of these natural adjustments some experts believe that a church develops a safe zone or comfort zone. Much like the oversized keel on a sail boat allows the boat to tilt several degrees in either direction without tipping over, many older, established churches consistently shift up or down in attendance and over time develop a comfort zone that allows them to feel safe.

For instance, suppose a congregation of twenty-five senior adults discovers a plateau in attendance. Every Sunday the regular attendees come to worship, but few, if any guests and no new members are part of the congregation. They are alarmed and realize that something has to change. Meanwhile, another congregation of twenty-five in average attendance may show the same statistical plateau but they frequently experience the loss of a few members and the addition of few new members. This church's sustained plateau may not be as alarming because the arrival of new members gives the congregation the illusion of growth. But in reality nothing has changed; the church is not growing.

Life Cycle Stages Measured by Attitudes

In the birth/re-birth to early growth years of the life cycle the congregation will be driven by the organizing vision. In the case of a new church this vision will often be framed and articulated by the founding pastor and early members. As the church seeks to establish healthy patterns of operation, all the ministries are closely aligned with the basic values and mission that brought it into existence. Generally, the structures of ministry at this stage are rather fluid, and formal outreach or discipleship ministries may not yet exist.

As the church moves to the growth stage of the life cycle, a passion develops to fulfill the organizing vision which results in more organized structures for ministry. A well-developed assimilation or inclusion strategy points new believers and new members on a clearly defined path to discipleship and participation. Structures are more formalized with stated preferences for worship style and a clear understanding of the basic values and belief systems that characterize the church. The drive to include more and more people in ministry, and the growth that results, often confront the congregation with the need for adequate facilities.

During the stages of birth and growth it is appropriate for the church to refine its vision and define its mission, since these features will propel the church for a generation or more. When the vision is well refined and the mission or purpose of the church is directly tied to the Great Commission, those early years of birth and growth establish a solid foundation that still allows for flexibility and adaptability across the years. A church can find itself in real trouble later if it is established with the primary vision of promoting a denominational identity, or if it is tied to a mission of gathering up disenfranchised or disgruntled members from other churches. When a church's mission is not in line with the Great Commission, that church will probably not exist for more than one or two generations.

As the church reaches maturity the congregation is in its prime with successful ministries run by committed leaders and active members. There is confidence in the future and it seems as if the sky is the limit for this thriving congregation. People are easily connected and involved. Individual spiritual growth is obvious. The worship services are well-liked and considered to be above average. Attendance reaches an all-time-high and a good reputation extends into the community. Ministry structures that provide a way to formally manage the congregation work well. Finances are strong, but the congregation begins to see its average age creep up as young adults move away and fewer young families are part of the congregation.

When a congregation finds itself in the cycle of full maturity or at the beginning stages of plateau, it is very important that the vision and mission of the church should be further refined, clarified, and expressed in contemporary terms. Society changes so rapidly that it can be very difficult to maintain relevance and connectedness to the current generation. Ideally, at maturity the leaders of the congregation will find the needed assistance, through such avenues as continuing education and church health assessments, to refocus as a means toward a new period of growth and development.

The church that reaches the life cycle stage of plateau will find that the vision or dream that called the congregation into existence is no longer as obvious as it once was. The congregation becomes more passive, with a focus on how to maintain the status quo. With this focus there is a reluctance to engage in new initiatives that involve risk-taking. Generally, the church that is plateaued will find the fastest growing demographic group to be senior adults, with a noticeable plateau or decline in children and youth under eighteen years of age. Morale declines, as the focus is more on maintaining a hold on past gains than on the exciting possibilities of the future.

Should a congregation find itself well into the cycle of plateau and suffering from initial decline, the process of refocus may assist in the evaluation of existing ministries and the formation of new ones that can lead to a new period of growth and development. The process can be more difficult at this point since the plateau and initial decline may limit the financial and personal resources needed for the new venture. Everyone capable of doing ministry may already be occupied with the existing ministries. Further, the mindset or attitudes of the congregation may not allow the group to view the situation with enough urgency to take necessary action.

As you might guess from the name of the next stage, when the church moves into decline there will be an obvious decline in worship attendance. The quality of ministries being offered declines and many of these ministries begin to disintegrate due to lack of attendance and loss of willing volunteers. There is an expressed desire to find new programs but little creative energy to make these new programs work.

Decline will frequently lead to nostalgia and the resulting blame-casting. Finances will generally shrink as attendance declines. There may be reduced confidence in the pastor's ability to provide effective leadership and pastoral turnover may occur. Dysfunction, that inability to sustain healthy relationships, begins to creep in, with the result that the church is no longer a good place to invite friends.

If decline continues the church will move into the drop-out stage of the life cycle. At this point people begin to drop out of ministry positions, often with little advance notice. With no ready pool of volunteers, positions may go unfilled. With a reduced income base, the congregation is afraid to take any risks that might diminish the few resources that are left. The congregation can become an old-age congregation with the most significant numbers of constituents being those who are home-bound or confined to nursing homes. As long as some resources are available, these old-age congregations have the ability to survive long past the time they are able to provide meaningful ministry to the community.

When the congregation moves to the life cycle stage of death, the church is subsistence level and may require outside support or internally generated endowments to maintain what ministry is present. The pastor will generally be bi-vocational and the remnant congregation often suffers from very low morale. The church exists as a preaching station, with its only ministry being that of a weekly worship service and a chaplaincy ministry for those who once were active participants.

Why Not Fight To Stay Open?

A large number of American churches are struggling with the hard questions of survival. Many churches across the nation are now faced with the unpleasant reality that they are only one major building repair away from being unable to sustain any visible presence in the community. Still other churches are faced with the unpleasant reality that the death or disability of one or two faithful members will completely cripple the church's ability to do ministry.

The purpose of this book, however, is not to paint a dismal picture of the inevitable closure of a large number of struggling churches that find themselves in the final stages of their life cycle. The purpose of this book is to pave the way for a legacy to be created so that the spirit and purpose of a faithful church might be carried on even if the worshipping congregation cannot be sustained. How might this happen? It happens best when the congregation and its leaders prayerfully and carefully seek the Lord's leading, recognizing their placement in the life cycle and taking appropriate steps in response.

When a congregation finds itself in steep decline or drop-out options are very limited. In the face of steep decline, the congregation may only have two options from which to choose.

Option one: Survive at all costs

When faced with a threatening, hostile environment the western-moving pioneers would stop their forward progress and circle their wagons to establish a defensive perimeter. This circle-the-wagon, maintenance type of ministry can often reduce program costs to a very low level by deferring building maintenance, cutting back on the weekly schedule, or providing for limited pastoral services. Many churches have reserve funds accumulated over the years that they will use to subsidize the currently minimal operation of the church.

This option, however convenient, does not provide a long-term solution for the troubled church. Such a circle-the-wagons approach may delay, but cannot prevent, the inevitable. It also does not fulfill the work of the Great Commission.

Option two: Become a legacy church

When faced with steep decline or drop-out, some congregations have faced the harsh realities and made the tough choices necessary to constructively deal with them. The brave leaders of these churches have put into practice the proverbial wisdom of the Lakota tribal elders: The best way to ride a dead horse is to dismount.

The second option is one we hope you prayerfully consider. In fact, it is the focal point of this entire book: Become a legacy church! Help to create spiritual children and leave an eternal legacy through birthing a new church. Allow the last decision you make as a church to be one of life and not death.

Life Cycle Checklist

1. Using attendance figures for the past ten years, chart your church's average annual attendance. Do you see growth, plateau or decline?
2. Using the attendance figures from the last ten years, what is the low point and what is the high point indicated there? Will existence in this comfort or safety zone allow the church to thrive and develop? Or will existence here lead to life support and a lingering death? If your church attendance is currently at its low point for the previous ten years, does this indicate decline and drop-out? Can you survive the current trends?
3. What attitudes are prevalent among your members?
   - ❑ We are energized and excited about our new beginning and its new possibilities. (Birth to early growth)
   - ❑ We have to get things done and we've organized with effective structures to include new people and to establish new ministries. (Growth)
   - ❑ Everything is working well and it looks like the sky is the limit if present trends continue. (Maturity)
   - ❑ We're not really interested in anything new and we're sure proud of our senior adults. (Plateau)
   - ❑ Attendance is much lower than it used to be and many of our ministries have been discontinued since we do not have people to lead them. (Decline)
   - ❑ Many of our folks are considering leaving and have abruptly ended their volunteer roles in our ministries. (Drop-out)
   - ❑ We're barely getting by and it sure helps when some out-of-town members send a check. (Death)
4. Take a congregational Life-Cycle Survey. A sample of the survey can be found in Appendix III. For further information on how to compile a full 360-congregational survey and consultation, go to *www.legacychurches.com*.

CHAPTER SIX

How Do You Know When It May Be Time To Close?

Disclaimer: Some of what you read in this chapter will be very difficult, and in some ways, frustrating. We want you to understand that we are in no way discrediting or dismissing the work of the smaller church. God has, and still does use these churches in powerful ways. This chapter is meant to generate discussion and introspection among those who are attempting to discern the direction the Lord has for their church. Some will read this chapter and begin to carefully evaluate the life and ministry of their church. Others will discover rays of hope and avenues for growth, and a constructive path that may lead to a turnaround. This chapter is not intended to be the final word on evaluating when it is time to close. Rather, this chapter should be considered as a tool to help you address specific issues in the life and health of your church. We hope you will read this chapter with an open mind and heart.

Making the decision to close a church is not easy. Emotions will run high and a sense of failure may pervade the hearts and minds of those remaining. Sadly, many churches in the final stage of the life cycle close only when one individual is left to turn off the lights. Congregations tend to hold on as long as possible and exhaust all resources, even if little hope remains. So, how do you know when it's time to close? Besides your placement in the life cycle, what key markers will be present in the life of your church?

Every year about 1 percent of churches in America close their doors. That may sound like a small percentage, but it means more than 3,200 churches close every year. Suppose you belong to a group of 1000 churches, you could expect about 10 of your member churches to close in one year. In some parts of the United States, the upheaval caused by a steadily decreasing population and serious decline in employment opportunities means this rate is even higher. If a denomination, convention, or association of churches has not been actively pursuing the starting of new churches, entire groups of churches will age, decline, and close.

Six Indicators of Potential Closure

1. Public Worship Attendance Has Drastically Declined.

Weekly worship services provide the most visible public ministry of the church. Every church needs enough critical mass (that is, adequate attendance) to make it look, feel, and sound alive. When worship attendance drops consistently below those levels it is difficult for a church to continue. The minimum number needed to have a strong worship service will vary based on the cultural, social, and economic environment of the church. For instance, in a smaller church facility that seats eighty to one hundred, fifty to sixty people may fill the sanctuary and create a strong sense of well-being. In a larger building, designed to seat several hundred, fifty to sixty attendees will not generate the positive momentum necessary to retain newcomers.

Critical mass, reflected in adequate attendance, is necessary to create a lively environment. A guest who attends a service for the first time is not likely to return if the church is perceived to be dying. You know the phrase "First impressions are everything"? This applies to churches as well as people. Few of us would argue that the first impressions we had about an individual determined how we treated them, at least to begin with. We make decisions like this every day. These first impressions help us determine where we eat, where we shop, what kind of clothes we wear, and with whom we spend our time. So it shouldn't surprise us to consider that unchurched people use that same axiom when looking at our church.

Critical mass is also important to create a positive forward momentum in the church. That may not be comfortable to hear, but it is true. Think about it this way. If a fight breaks out on a busy street, what happens? People begin to gather and watch the battle. Once a crowd begins to form, it doesn't take long for a mob mentality to kick in and spiral out of control. That is why police officers try to disperse a crowd as quickly as possible. Crowds beget crowds.

We live in an over stimulated culture. Americans like to be in places where things are moving and shaking. If they perceive that your church is not one of those places, don't expect much enthusiasm. Of course, the ultimate goal of the local church is transformed lives, not just a large crowd. But lives can't be touched if people aren't showing up at church. We don't have to like that fact, we simply have to accept it. If your church hopes to grow, which should be the desire of every church, then you have to understand the culture in which we live.

Our culture is a culture of bigness. Big malls, huge parking lots, massive theaters, and enormous office buildings have become standard. Bigness has become an American axiom: "The bigger, the better!" It shouldn't surprise you that unchurched people carry this axiom to church. When they enter the doors of a church and it doesn't reflect the culture they live in they experience a disconnect.

A rough estimate of attendees necessary to create a good worship environment in any size church is thirty to fifty adults. (This number could be as low as thirty if the church is located in a very secluded, rural area.) A church that has only twenty to forty adults at worship puts itself in a potentially unhealthy situation. When fewer than twenty adults attend worship it may be very difficult for a church to survive long-term, unless corrective measures are taken. Less than twenty adults is a strong indication that the church, short of a powerful move of God, may not survive beyond the next decade. In some settings, depending on the gifts and graces of the members, these numbers may need to be adjusted to reflect the local context.

Ask yourself these questions:

A. How many adults attend your church each Sunday?

B. What is the attitude and atmosphere of the service?

C. What impressions might a visitor get upon walking in (Keep in mind that younger guests will think differently than older guests. If your church is going to grow you will need plenty of young families.)

D. Based on the seating patterns of the auditorium, how many people are needed to make the room look comfortably full? (In many declining churches the worshipping congregation often clusters in the back rows, seriously detached from the worship event.)

2. Staffing of Essential Ministries Is No longer Adequate or Effective.

In order for a ministry to function, it must not only have adequate staff, it must also have effective staff. It is one thing to have enough bodies to fill needed ministry positions, it is quite another to have the properly gifted and skilled leaders to provide effective ministry. As a church declines, the nature and ability of the congregation changes. It may be possible to have a large enough group to meet every ministry need of the church without having the gifts and skills necessary to function effectively. Much of the time churches that fit into this category have two or three workaholics who wear multiple hats. Conventional wisdom tells us that 20 percent of the people, do 80 percent of the work. That is called the 80/20 rule. In churches experiencing decline the rule shifts to look more like 90/10. That means in a church of fifty, five are doing the bulk of the work. Usually those people are the pastor, his wife, and one other couple or family.

The lack of workers needed to operate the church speeds its decline. If a church is to have any hope of reversing its steady decline, volunteers will be needed to run the basic ministries of the church: pianist, bookkeeper, nursery workers, Sunday school teachers, and children's workers. Yet, as the church declines, so does the volunteer base.

How many workers are really necessary to run effective ministries? The National Association for the Education of Young Children suggests that a proper learning environment for children includes an adult/child ratio of one adult for every three children twenty-three months and younger, one adult for every four children twenty-four to thirty months old, and one adult for every five children thirty-one to thirty-six months old.[17] As the child gets older, the ratio changes but the need remains for a number of qualified workers. Within the small group arena, conventional wisdom teaches that an adult small group should have no more than twelve adults per leader.

Maybe your church is doing well with these ratios. But, if a church is to experience growth, it will have to do more than just sustain its internal ministry. Almost twenty years ago Win Arn shared with the Christian world that for every three workers helping to maintain the internal ministry of the church, one was needed to execute effective outreach and evangelism.[18] When a church is struggling to gather enough people just to sustain its internal ministries, it is not able to offer effective ministries to the community and the chances of growth are slim.

Ask yourself these questions:

A. Do we have enough people in the church to do ministry well?

B. Are some in the church doing more than their fair share? Is that because the church is doing too much, or because not enough workers are available?

C. Does our current ministry structure provide the ability to grow, if God chooses to send us guests?

D. Can we provide effective ministries to the community or are most of our ministries inwardly focused?

3. Annual Income Is No Longer Adequate To Do Effective Local Ministry.

To sustain the ministries of the church a certain level of minimum income is necessary. Ministry requires money. There is no way to get around that statement. Effective ministry requires more! Although the minimum income required for maintenance and basic operations will vary from one location to another, church budgets are generally built around salaries, building operations, and outreach to the community. Unfortunately, many churches spend the vast majority of the annual budget on their facility, leaving little, if any, money for effective outreach

17. These statistics will vary from state to state. More information can be obtained at: http://www.ncrel.org/sdrs/areas/issues/students/earlycld/ea1lk7-1.htm.
18. Win Arn, *The Church Growth Ratio Book: How to Have a Revitalized, Healthy, Growing, Loving Church,* (Monrovia, CA: Church Growth Inc., 1990), page 64.

and evangelism. What little money declining churches do have left is used to severely underpay a bi-vocational pastor.

Financial needs will also differ according to the different socio-economic setting of the church. For instance, a church in a rural setting may require much less financial support to keep it functioning than a church in the middle of a major metropolitan setting. Even the geographic location of the church can have an effect on the necessary finances needed to do ministry well. In Northern Michigan, for instance, heating costs can be much higher than a church in a more moderate southern state. So how much does it take to adequately resource a church?

If the church intends to pay the pastor a full-time salary with benefits, which we highly recommend, the church will need anywhere from ten to fifteen tithing families to provide adequate support. This package includes a base salary, housing or a housing allowance, health insurance, and a basic pension plan. If the church chooses to engage a bi-vocational pastor the number of families required to fund that pastor's support would be reduced to seven to eleven families. Again, this all depends on the cost of living in your area.

In addition to paying the pastor, the church will also need another five to ten or more tithing families to pay the utilities, provide basic maintenance, stock cleaning supplies, and purchase property insurance. The matter of building operations often finds a struggling congregation coping with a large building that is rarely used and in need of major repairs.

So, a church with a full-time pastor needs a bare minimum of fifteen tithing families just to pay the pastor, keep the lights on and maintain the facility. In a bi-vocational setting the church will need a bare minimum of twelve tithing families. If maintenance ministries were all God commissioned the Church to do, everything would be fine. However, we are called to be on a co-mission with Him. We are called to "go and make disciples of all nations" (Matt. 28:19). That co-mission involves many other activities, such as evangelism, outreach, advertising, and global missions work.

Some churches find themselves committed to denominational apportionments or international missionary support they have agreed to undertake. As a result, these churches may be financially obligated to give what may equal at least one family's annual tithe. That is not to say that apportionments are bad, they are just another factor in the equation.

If the congregation desires to grow and remain healthy it will have to spend at least 5 percent of its annual budget engaging the local community with the gospel of Christ. Investing in "the ends of the earth" is a biblically necessary ministry. Unfortunately, many congregations have forgotten to invest in their own "Jerusalem."

Having summarized the financial needs of the congregation, we can now project the minimum number of tithing families needed to meet the financial needs of a church.

Item	**Range of tithing families needed**
Salary and benefits full-time/part time	10 - 15 / 7-11
Building and grounds	5 - 10
Missions	1 - 5
Local Ministries	2 - 5

Using the chart above, the minimum number of tithing families needed to underwrite the ministries of a church, depending on the cost of living and doing business in your setting, would range from 18 to 35 for a church with a full-time pastor and 15 to 31 for a church with a bi-vocational pastor.

Hidden dangers

There are a few factors that can disguise the financial realities of a church. Sometimes a church is fortunate to have generous givers who contribute large amounts of money. This can become a very serious problem if the generous donor is no longer able, or willing, to give at that level. It is much better for a church to rely on faithful giving from many families than from a few exceptionally generous givers.

Deferred building maintenance may also disguise the financial realities of the congregation. Nevertheless, heating and air conditioning equipment does eventually break down or wear out. Roofing systems will eventually need to be replaced. Parking lots and plumbing will eventually require attention. When the need arise to address the aging equipment, the repair costs can be devastating for a church in decline.

In some settings a denominational subsidy may prolong the life of a struggling congregation. Grants to cover many of the routine costs of ministry may be developed. So, for a period of time all seems to be well. The end of the grant cycle, however, brings the stark reality that effective, Great Commission ministry costs money and that local church ministries must be funded locally.

Ask yourself these questions:

A. How many tithing families do we have in the church?

B. Does giving in your church accomplish more than simply maintaining our present facility?

C. Does giving in your church enable Great Commission work?

D. What will it take, financially speaking, for your church to do proper ministry in the community?

E. If growth doesn't happen in the church, how long will reserves last? When will your spending become an act of self-indulgence instead of ministry?

4. The Church Has Not Consistently Grown Over the Last Five Years.

As we pointed out in chapter three, periods of plateau and decline are natural in the life cycle of all churches. When a one or two year period of decline is reversed by renewed growth, these short periods of decline are of concern but they are not alarming in and of themselves. Long periods of decline or plateau however, should be a loud warning of potential closure.

In the United States, 1 percent of the population dies annually. By contrast, the annual birth rate is around 1.4 percent of the population. As a result, the United States population is increasing every year. If these percentages were reversed, the United States would be experiencing decline. A local church is no different. A church will experience growth when the rate of conversions, baptisms, and membership transfers exceeds the rate of members who pass away, move away, become ill, or simply no longer attend. The church declines when the number of members who die, move away, or no longer attend, exceeds new members brought in. The longer a church experiences decline, the harder it will be to stop the negative momentum.

A typical church will lose 6 to 10 percent of their attendees every year. If a church is to grow, it will need to experience a steady influx of new faces. About 5 percent of your weekly attendance should be made up of first-time guests. Of those guests, the church will need to retain at least 1 out of every 4. In 1990 Win Arn published *The Church Growth Ratio Book.* Among other findings, Arn discovered "declining churches see only 10-12% of their first time visitors eventually join. Slightly growing churches will see 14-16% of first time visitors join. Significantly growing churches with an intentional priority on attracting and following up on newcomers see 25% or more of their first time visitors join and integrated into the church within the first year."[19]

Congregations that are able to adjust to the changing culture and effectively relate to the context of their community will begin to reverse the effects of decline. A local congregation really only has two choices: change how they relate to the community, or move to a place where their style of ministry fits the context.

Ask yourself these questions:

A. Have we grown over the last 5 years? (Open your records and begin to trace your growth or decline pattern.)

B. How many visitors have we had over the last five years? What does that average out to per week? What is the visitor/member ratio per week?

C. What percentage of our first-time visitors return for a second and third visit?

D. How willing are we to change the way we do church?

5. The Age or Tenure of the Membership Is Unusually High.

When a congregation is composed almost exclusively of people much older than the average age of the local population, crossing the age barrier becomes very difficult. When the congregation is composed only of long-term members, they tend to form cliques and close themselves off to new members. When both of these circumstances are present in a church, long-term survival will be extremely difficult.

The landscape of America is dotted with churches that fit this description. These churches are composed of aging members who have

19. Arn, The Church Growth Ratio Book, page 50.

been attending the church for thirty or more years. In the Presbyterian denomination, the average age of a member is fifty-eight. In the United Methodist denomination, the average member is sixty-one. The Episcopalians don't fair much better. Ninety-eight percent of their members are over the age of 50.[20]

In contrast, the median age in the United States is about 37 years old. While the average age of a local community can vary significantly from the national average, the point is simple: in order to grow you must have younger families continually joining the church.

Why do these two factors make it so hard to grow? 1) Older members tend not to embrace change. 2) Longtime members tend to have an overdeveloped and unhealthy sense of ownership over the church. 3) When a church is made up of older adults, children are not usually a part of their family structure, which limits the future of the church.

When a congregation is aging more rapidly than its community, and it is not bringing in new members, long-term survival is unlikely.

Ask yourself these questions:

A. What is the average age of your membership?

B. What is the average tenure of your members?

C. How many young families are an active part of the church?

6. Survival Has Become The Main Mission.

Just before Jesus ascended into heaven He shared the Great Commission with his disciples. He said, "Go and make disciples of all nations, baptizing them in the name of the Father and of the Son and of the Holy Spirit, and teaching them to obey everything I have commanded you." (Matt. 28:19-20.) Seems pretty straightforward and simple, doesn't it? The mission Jesus gave to His followers/Church was to share the good news, baptize new believers, and teach them how to live as believers. Healthy, growing churches are effectively engaged in all three aspects of the Great Commission.

Unfortunately, churches in the final stages of the life cycle often exchange the Great Commission for a mission of survival. This exchange isn't something that takes place overnight, nor is it done with intentional malice. Usually this exchange happens when churches experience

20. David T. Olson, The American Church in Crisis: Groundbreaking Research Based on a National Database of over 200,000 Churches (Grand Rapids: Zondervan, 2008) page 85.

loss of attendance or membership, coupled with an inability to meet financial obligations and ministry needs. When every ministry of the church is self-serving and every dollar is used to keep the doors open, this indicates that a survival mentality has set in.

The more decline a church experiences the more tenaciously it may fight to survive. Instead of a healthy outward focus, the congregation turns inward, cuts off all non-essential spending (that usually means everything but the bills), and tries to weather the storm. Ministry ceases while the congregation waits for growth to occur once again. Yet, without ministry to the outside world, that growth rarely happens. So the church stays in a perpetual mode of survival. Some churches see their ability to survive as a badge of honor, yet nothing could be further from the original mission of the church. In fact, as a church begins to experience decline, instead of circling the wagons, they should renew a commitment to reach out to the community.

There are two large bodies of water in Israel. One is teaming with life and the other is dead, yet the same stream feeds both bodies of water. What is the difference? One body, the Sea of Galilee, takes water in and sends water out. The other body of water, the Dead Sea only receives water. When a church, for the sake of survival, stops reaching out to the community, long-term survival will be extremely difficult.

Ask yourself these questions:

A. When did our church last experience growth by conversion?

B. How much of our spending is devoted to keeping the doors open and how much is invested in missions and evangelism? (Expressing these as percentages may be more helpful than expressing them as dollar figures.)

C. What effective ministry do we offer to our community?

SELF-TEST

This diagnostic self-test is very simple and not intended to be an exhaustive indicator of the health of your church. It should not, however, be taken lightly. Once you have finished, use the score key below to foster open dialogue in your congregation.

	YES	NO
1. Do you have critical mass for Sunday morning worship?	___	___
2. Do you have more than thirty adults in worship on Sunday morning?	___	___
3. Do you have enough staff/volunteers to do effective ministry?	___	___
4. Do you have at least one individual doing external evangelism for every three people doing internal ministry?	___	___
5. Do you have at least fifteen (for churches with a bi-vocational pastor) or eighteen (for churches with a full-time pastor) tithing families in the church?	___	___
6. Does your actual spending include at least 5 percent towards outreach and evangelism in the local community?	___	___
7. Have you grown by 5 percent each year over the last five years?	___	___
8. Are you retaining at least 16 percent of your first time visitors?	___	___
9. Is the average age of your membership less than thirty to fifty? *(This average depends a great deal on the setting of the church.)*	___	___
10. Is the average tenure of your membership over thirty years?	___	___
11. Does the church have frequent conversions/baptisms?	___	___
12. If you were to be honest, is the main focus of the church outward? *(Do you have resources you won't spend? Are most of your programs for the already saved?)*	___	___

Score: Each YES is worth 2 points. **24 points are possible**.

0 -- 10	Should consider becoming a legacy church.
12 – 16	Change is needed now to insure survival.
18 – 20	A few minor adjustments could help your church experience revival.
22 – 24	The church is functioning as it should.

CHAPTER SEVEN

Understanding the Process of Closing a Church

Congregations are often left to themselves as they figure out how to proceed beyond the initial decision to close. Many struggle to understand what to do next. What do you do with the property? What are the legal requirements for closing a church? What do you do with bank accounts, endowments, gifts, and the like? How can you ensure the vision of your founders is honored and continued? If you belong to a denominational family, someone other than the congregation will more than likely handle these decisions. If you are an autonomous congregation, or if your denominational structure places that authority in the hands of the local body, this chapter is designed to help answer these kinds of questions by providing a basic outline to help you close with integrity.

While this chapter may seem a little tedious, we hope it will help ease the frustrations that can occur while trying to wrap up the ministry life of your church.

Calling the Final Meeting

Every church will differ on how to make this decision. Due to the seriousness of the action, most churches will require a properly called business meeting. You will have to check your church's bylaws to determine if this is necessary. If you call a meeting of this nature make sure adequate time is provided to notify every member. Usually, announcing a meeting from the pulpit two to four weeks prior will be sufficient.

Keep in mind that you may have members still on your roll who no longer attend. Invite these members as well. Even though they may not show up for the meeting, a failure to invite them could cause unwanted problems in the future. For instance, if your church bylaws require you to inform all members of a congregational meeting two weeks in advance and you do not do so, those members may be able to legally challenge any decision because they were not properly notified. If your membership rolls haven't been updated recently and you have people on the rolls that haven't attended for years, you are not alone. Thousands of churches across the United States have a dwindling attendance and inflated membership rolls. That just means you have to be extra cautious when making any decision that requires the entire membership to approve.

Once the meeting has been properly called and everyone invited, the congregation will have several collective decisions to make. Prior to conducting this final meeting the church leadership should review the church's Articles of Incorporation, and the church Constitution and Bylaws to see if there are any special requirements. The best policy is to be as prepared as possible because this meeting will already be difficult enough. A failure to be prepared could drag the meeting on or cause it to fail altogether.

What if your church does not have a set of bylaws or organizing documents? That is not as strange a question as you may think. Many established churches across our nation have been operating without bylaws and governing documents since the day they were birthed. If your church does not have bylaws you will have to govern your meeting according to your standard, accepted practices. How do you know what your "standard practices" are? Simply follow the process you have always used to make business decisions within the church. If you are part of a denominational family, use the standard forms and practices that have been outlined for your organization.

Conducting the Final Meeting

Here is a brief outline for conducting a meeting.

1. Start with devotions and prayer

The church may be closing, but it is still a body of believers and God is still God. Make sure that everything you do is covered with His power and presence. Use the Scripture to help the congregation understand that God's truth marches on, even in the midst of great pain and frustration. After the loss of Moses, the people of Israel were about to cross the Jordan River. God told them, "I will never leave you nor forsake you" (Josh. 1:5).

2. Share the reason for the meeting

Spend adequate time helping the congregation understand why the church is closing. The leadership team, deacon board, elder board, or official board (whatever term you use) should meet prior to the congregational gathering and offer its recommendations. Voting on the recommendations made by the leadership team should improve credibility. These recommendations should assure the congregation that they are not voting to close the church due to personal reasons, emotional instability of the pastor, or the whim of a few power brokers of the church. We recommend you use the "motion and approval" methods outlined by Robert's Rules of Order.

3. Make a decision for distribution of the assets

This will probably be one of the most difficult items to tackle. Every member will have an idea for the use of the church's property and assets. (More on that later.) If the congregation trusts the leadership, it may be wise to make a recommendation that the leadership handle this responsibility. Giving the leadership authority to disburse the assets will save you hours of discussion and frustration.

4. Plan for a final "Celebration Service"

No church should be allowed to slip quietly into oblivion. We can't emphasize this enough. Take time to celebrate what God has done. Every church has left an eternal footprint on its community. Make sure you celebrate that faithfulness. Invite the community. Invite the local paper! Do not allow your community to forget the love and commitment your church has shown throughout the years.

5. Close the meeting with a time of sharing, but keep it positive!

Make time for those who have attended the meeting to share their memories. This can be a powerful ending to a painful evening. Allowing your remaining members to openly express their feelings is a wonderfully healing process. It will also offer them an opportunity for personal closure.

Whatever you decide to do for this final meeting, make sure someone is taking detailed notes. A copy of these final minutes, with a listing of how all assets will be distributed, will need to be sent to any entity receiving a portion of the assets. The more detailed your note-taking during this last meeting, the less opportunity for any misunderstandings.

What Do We Do with the Church Assets?

Determining how to dispose of the church's property, assets and remaining finances can be an enormous project. By "dispose of" we do not mean "throw away." Disposing of assets means to "give away." Deciding how to handle the assets does not have to be hard, but it must be handled thoughtfully. Many items in a church carry sentimental value for some. Determining how to dispose of those memorabilia in an orderly way can cause damaging rifts between longtime friends.

The Internal Revenue Service has strict guidelines for the disposing of non-profit assets. According to the IRS:

> Assets of an organization must be permanently dedicated to an exempt purpose. This means that should an organization dissolve, its assets must be distributed for an exempt purpose described in this chapter, or to the federal government or to a state or local government for a public purpose. If the assets could be distributed to members or private individuals or for any other purpose, the organizational test is not met.[21]

In other words, once something is given to a church, it belongs solely to the church. If a church closes, where these items go is to be determined by the remaining members. You cannot open the door and allow a free-for-all. No one individual can come back and say, "I bought that for the church, so I want it back."

Another important aspect of the non-profit tax code is also found in Section 501(c)(3) under the "Dissolution" clause. If a church decides to close its doors, it is **required** to dispose of the remaining assets by transferring them to other charities with **like charitable purposes**. "No

21. This is found under the rules for an IRS section 501(c)(3) organization, chapter 3. http://www.irs.gov/publications/p557/ch03.html#d0e3402.

part of the net earnings of the corporation shall inure to the benefit of, or be distributable to its members, trustees, officers, or other private persons." Helping your congregation to understand these two rules may save a lot of trouble. It will also help in determining which charities will qualify to receive the church's assets.

For instance, you may decide to give everything to a neighboring church, or to your local association, convention, or denomination. Any of these choices would fit within the boundaries of a "like purposes" organization. However, organizations like the American Red Cross, the United Way, or a local school or hospital will not qualify. The services these organizations offer may be wonderful, but their purpose is not the same. Besides, you should always be careful to preserve the original intention of the church founders. Previous members did not give money to the church so it could go to an organization that doesn't support the same spiritual mission.

We have tried to make the case that one of the best ways to handle the church's assets is to give them to a church planting organization. There is no better way to leave a legacy than to fund the beginning of a new work! How is that leaving a legacy? Imagine what might happen if your church's last action was to fund the start of a new church. New churches are notably efficient at winning people to Christ, raising up new leaders, and funding new missions across the world. By funding a church plant, the vision of your church is carried on through the life of this new ministry.

What kind of assets will have to be considered when closing a church?

A. Non-Fixed Assets, Knickknacks, and Memorabilia

Let's start with the easiest assets first. It is amazing the massive amounts of "stuff" a church can collect over the years. Over a lifetime, churches acquire pictures, photographs, posters, and a myriad of other religious decorations. The pews are often full of outdated hymnbooks, Bibles, offering envelopes, and visitor cards. Not to mention the storeroom where you place all your used VBS and Sunday School material. All of these items, as well as many other non-fixed assets, will need to be disposed of during closing.

Many of these items have little value to anyone but the present congregation. In this sense “dispose of” does mean “throw away.” But before taking that drastic step, keep in mind that some of these items may have no market value, but may possess great sentimental value to certain individuals in the congregation. For instance, a picture on the wall or a handmade cross hanging on the pulpit may have great value to the family members of the individual who donated the item. If these items have no market value, then you may consider allowing the family who donated the gifts to take them back. You may even have a few items in the church that hold historical significance to your denomination/group, or the community where the church is located. Your church is a matter of history so don’t be afraid to offer a few items to the local museum.

No matter what items you may have in the church, it is unlikely anyone will be interested in your old hymnbooks, outdated VBS and Sunday School material, broken music stands, torn and discolored choir robes, or children’s toys that look like they have gone through the meat grinder. It is better to throw these items away.

Every church will have a few valuable items they can sell such as pianos, organs, office furniture, audio/visual equipment, nursery items, outdoor play equipment, and possibly even the pews. If the church does not intend to donate this equipment to another church or church plant, each of these items should be appraised and sold at market value.

B. Properties and Buildings

For most churches, existing properties and buildings are their largest asset, and can become a major contribution. Before any decisions can be made concerning the property, it is necessary to look at the deed. In some cases a deed will contain a reversion clause. A reversion clause will contain important information about what a congregation can or cannot do with a piece of property.

For instance, the property may have been given to the church by one of the founding leaders. That leader may have placed a stipulation on the property about its usage. If the church closes, the reversion clause may require the property to revert back to the donor or donor’s family. The reversion clause may even have detailed stipulations about how the property is to be divided. So, before your congregation can decide what to do with a piece of property, the deed must be consulted.

If a reversion clause does not exist on the deed, your church is free to proceed. Two different paths can be followed to dispose of the property.

1. You can choose to sell it yourself or through a local realtor. If you choose this path, you will have to determine, prior to the sale, the price and how the money will be distributed.
2. You can give the church to your association, convention, denomination, or another church, and let them deal with the details. If you choose to go this route, make sure the organization receiving the property understands the purpose of the gift and honors your donation wishes.

C. Official Records

Make sure that every decision your congregation makes about closing is carefully detailed and saved. You may need to refer to these records at some point in the future. Below are three kinds of items you will need to keep for archival purposes. If you are independent and have no family-type group, have someone in your church place these records in storage for at least three years. All financial records must be kept for at least seven years in the event that they are needed to provide information to the IRS.

1. Membership Records

Once the church closes, every member or attendee will be looking for a new church to call home. Do your members a favor and make sure your membership records are up to date. Keep your membership roll open as long as possible in order to give your people time to find a new church home. Send out a letter to each of them explaining the decision to close and how they are able to get a letter of transfer.

It may be best to have the board write a form letter explaining the situation, and give it to the members so they can present it to a church that requires a letter of transfer. Most churches today will require a newcomer to attend a new member class, so the letter of transfer may not be an issue. Remember, the loss of church family will be difficult, so do everything within your power to make this transition as smooth as possible for your faithful members.

Make sure to place a current copy of members in the files you send to your parent organization.

2. Official Minutes

By official minutes we mean any documents that pertain to the business of the church. These come from committees and boards like trustees, leadership team, official board, finance committee, etc. These documents contain important information about the business of the church and the decisions made while still in operation. These documents should be protected in order to ensure the integrity of the church's decisions.

3. Office Files

The offices files may be personal in nature. They may contain annual calendars, budgets, and other personal files. These files may or may not be important to a congregation upon closing. If you belong to a denominational family, they may request a copy of these records. If you are an independent congregation, these records may not be as important. In either case, it is wise to keep a copy of all insurance policies, maintenance records, and equipment warrantees.

As mentioned above, it is very important that the congregation keep an archived record of the church finances for seven years. These records include a copy of the budgets, ledgers, bank deposits, checkbook, bank statements, cancelled checks, annual audits, and receipts. Why keep these records? The IRS may wish to audit the closing of your 501(c)(3). Archiving your records will save you an immense amount of difficulty if this happens.

D. Bank Accounts, Endowments, Memorials, and Specified Gifts

Of all the issues a congregation will face while closing, this is often the most difficult. While closing a bank account is relatively easy, many churches have multiple accounts with varying purposes. Many of these extra accounts carry specific restrictions for the uses of the funds. For instance, a church may have been given a large sum of money by a deceased member for a new educational wing. Since the congregation has decided to close, this gift will not be utilized for the intended purpose. Where does the money go? It may be necessary to involve an attorney in this process.

Any remaining assets from bequests, endowments or memorials will need to be handled carefully. In some cases, the donors may need to be contacted before any monies can be released. Depending on how involved these assets are, it may take some time before all of the assets can be properly transferred to another church, church plant, or denominational entity.

E. Federal/State Paperwork

A few federal and state papers may need to be completed to officially close out the church's incorporation. These papers include the church's Employee Identification Number (E.I.N.), state incorporation, and federal tax exemption.

1. Federal Papers

If the church has a pastor, secretary, treasurer, or any other employee on the payroll and is withholding federal taxes for these employees, a final Form 941 will need to be completed. Part 3, question 16 will ask you if this is the final tax return. Follow the instructions on the page. This should close out your E.I.N. If you do not fill this return out properly, you will continue to receive tax papers from the IRS. Your final filing of the 941 form should also notify the IRS that your 501(c)(3) has dissolved.

2. State Papers

Every state will have a different avenue for officially dissolving your incorporation. The best way to find out your state's requirements is to call, or go online to your Secretary of State's office. In most states, you will be required to fill out a dissolution statement and send it back to the Secretary of State's office for archiving. As with the federal papers, if you fail to do this, the church will continue to receive mail and be liable as a recognized non-profit organization within your state.

Where Should the Assets Go?

When all is said and done, where is the best place for a closing church to invest its assets? As long as the recipient falls in line with the original intention of the church, the possibilities are endless. However, some possibilities are better than others. Here are five of them:

1) Leave your assets to another local congregation. Provided the congregation is healthy and growing, that may be a very wise choice. It does not, however, ensure your legacy. Don't just give your assets away to another congregation that has no pattern of growth or history of conversion.

2) Consider leaving your assets to a Christian university, to have a building named after your church. A nice idea, but the reason for a name on a building will soon be forgotten. One generation later, few will remember a thing about your church.

3) Leave everything to a local Christian homeless shelter or mission. This is another great idea, but your donation will be just one of many.

4) Leave everything to your association, convention or denomination. In many cases this decision will help your group/family move forward for a short period. Often these entities use the extra money to fill budgetary shortfalls. It may even alleviate temporary financial strain, but in the end it has no legacy effect.

5) Use your assets to start another church. This is the avenue we recommend. Using your assets to start another church is the best way to guarantee your ministry legacy will live on. Giving birth to a child ensures the continuation of the family name. In that same vein, a congregation giving birth to a new church will ensure that the vision and ministry of the church will live on through the new work. We call this kind of giving "a history with a future."

Every congregation must wrestle with questions when deciding where to invest their final assets. How can the assets best serve the Kingdom of God? What will be the best way to invest the assets for future expansion? How will our investment make a difference in the lives of future believers? Ministry doesn't have to end when a church closes its doors.

CHAPTER EIGHT

The Final Chapter

If your church is in the final stages of its life cycle, we hope the information within these pages has been helpful. As this book draws to a close, we want to offer a few practical suggestions for developing a final celebration service. This service, if planned well, can leave a lasting testimony in the community. This service should be designed to give current members a chance to say goodbye and to create a healthy sense of closure. It will also show the surrounding community that God's truth still marches on. These suggestions will help your church close with dignity and create a sense of hope for the future.

1. Use the media.

Publicize the closing of your church as much as possible. Don't pass up the opportunity to invite the local newspaper, TV station, or radio station to the closing service. A quick read through the local paper or a few minutes watching the evening news will reveal that the media loves gloom-and-doom stories. So, your seemingly heartbreaking story of a dying church will appeal to them. This may sound counterproductive or even foolish, but a powerful, strategic, celebratory service can turn a painful story into one of hope and promise. How your church handles this service can speak volumes to the community. Don't allow your church to quietly slip away.

2. Invite all current and former members.

Send an invitation to every living individual who has been a member of the church. Funerals have a way of bringing together family and friends who haven't seen each other in years. Use this phenomenon to your advantage. When large crowds gather to celebrate the passing of an individual you will hear people in the crowd say, "Wow, he meant a lot to many people!" or, "She must have touched a lot of lives." That is the kind of atmosphere you want to create as well. Imagine what an impact that testimony would have on the community.

3. Invite the recipients of your church's assets.

If your church has already decided where its assets should go and the leaders of the recipient church or denomination are able to come, invite them to be a part of the service. As shared in a previous chapter, the Evangelical Covenant Church has a celebration and passes a baton. We suggest you do something similar with the leaders of the new church. This symbolism will help everyone present realize that this is not the end of the church's influence, but the beginning. If at all possible, ask the leaders of the new church to come forward at the end of the service, lay hands on them, and commission them to do God's work.

4. Allow a time of sharing.

Invite several members to share how the church impacted their lives. Once several planned times of sharing have been completed, open the floor for the attendees to share. You may be surprised to find out that the church affected people's lives in ways you never imagined. Whatever you do, make sure you set an unofficial (keep it to yourself) time frame for sharing. If you don't set a limit, you may unintentionally have a three-hour service that wears everyone down. A long and drawn-out service can have the opposite effect of what was desired.

5. Share the plan of becoming a legacy church.

Don't pass up the opportunity to share the church's plan to leave a legacy. Take the time to explain why leaving a legacy is so important. Weave together a powerful story of how your church will enable another to be birthed. Help everyone to see how your church's sacrifice will ultimately contribute to the salvation of hundreds through the ministry of a new church plant. You never know who will be in the crowd. Several pastors or leaders from other congregations may be facing tough times in their own church. Your commitment and vision to leave a legacy may inspire them to do the same.

6. Create a meaningful service with a positive flow.

Creating a positive flow for a final service can be difficult. The tendency may be to pack the final service with as much content as possible. Keep in mind that too much content can cloud the purpose of the service and create frustration instead of meaning. Here are a few suggested orders of service to help stimulate your mind as you prepare for the final service. Each of the following services are basically the same, with a few minor differences.

A) The Closing Service as a Final Homecoming.

Many churches will still be in contact with former members or attendees who were positively impacted by the life and ministry of the church. If invited, many of these former members will be willing to come back for a final homecoming. If this is the case it would be wise to utilize some of them as participants in the final service. You should also consider inviting members of other churches in the community. An order of service that includes this feature might flow in the following manner:

Prelude

Welcome (Explain the special nature of this service.)

Call to Worship

Invocation/Opening Prayer (Focus this prayer as one of thanksgiving for the life and ministry of the church.)

Congregational Music (Selections could be favorite songs of the congregation or could be selected to focus on the goodness and greatness of God. Possible hymns might include: "Great Is Thy Faithfulness", "How Great Thou Art", "All the Way My Savior Leads Me", "This Is My Father's World")

A Testimony to the Impact of this Church (This would be especially meaningful if offered by a former member who has returned for the final celebration.)

A Brief History of the Church (This should be no more than 3–5 minutes.)

Special Music (This would be especially meaningful if offered by a former member who has returned for the final celebration.)

Sermon (The sermon should focus on the ongoing mission of the church and could develop the theme of partnership in the larger mission as outlined in Philippians 1.)

Response (This could be done by congregational singing or by a special piece of music.)

Becoming a Legacy Church (A leader from the congregation should explain the decision of the church to continue its legacy and should indicate how that legacy will be realized.)

Accepting the Legacy (If a representative of the denomination is present, appropriate words of commendation and acceptance could be shared with the congregation.)

Closing Prayer (Led by the denominational representative who will invite the remaining members to come forward for this prayer time.)

The Final Benediction: Inasmuch as the congregation of ______________________ has chosen to end its public ministry and to continue that ministry through conveying it assets to ____________________________, I therefore declare that the public ministry of ________________________ has come to an end and that all remaining legal affairs of the congregation will be entrusted to the congregational leaders in keeping with the previous decision of the church. We give thanks to God for His grace that has blessed ____________________ with an effective ministry. We commend to Him the legacy bestowed this day by ___________________ and we ask that the Lord of the Church who has blessed and guided __________________ will continue to bless, guide, and prosper its legacy.

B) The Closing Service as a Final Celebration

If few guests are available to return for a homecoming celebration the congregation might consider the closing service as a final celebration. The service can be much shorter, but doesn't have to lack any elements. Denominational officials and/or legacy recipients should be invited to participate.

Prelude

Welcome (Explain the special nature of this service.)

Call to Worship

Invocation/Opening Prayer (Focus this prayer as one of thanksgiving for the life and ministry of the church.)

Congregational Music (Selections could be favorite songs of the congregation or could be selected to focus on the goodness and greatness of God. Possible hymns might include: “Great Is Thy Faithfulness”, “How Great Thou Art”, “All the Way My Savior Leads Me”, “This Is My Father’s World”.)

A Testimony to the Impact of this Church

A Brief History of the Church (This should be no more than 3–5 minutes.)

Special Music or a Congregational Song

Sermon (The sermon should focus on the ongoing mission of the church and could develop the theme of partnership in the larger mission as outlined in Philippians 1.)

Response The Lord’s Supper/Communion Service (Conducted in keeping with the traditions of the congregation. This small intimate Lord’s Supper Service can be a powerful reminder of the great things to come.)

Becoming a Legacy Church (A leader from the congregation should explain the decision of the church to continue its legacy and should indicate how that legacy will be realized.)

Accepting the Legacy (If a representative of the denomination is present, appropriate words of commendation and acceptance could be shared with the congregation.)

Closing Prayer (Led by the denominational representative who will invite the remaining members to come forward for this prayer time.)

The Final Benediction: Inasmuch as the congregation of ______________________ has chosen to end its public ministry and to continue that ministry through conveying it assets to ____________________________, I therefore declare that the public ministry of ______________________ has come to an end and that all remaining legal affairs of the congregation will be entrusted to the congregational leaders in keeping with the previous decision of the church. We give thanks to God for His grace that has blessed __________________ with an effective ministry. We commend to Him the legacy bestowed this day by __________________ and we ask that the Lord of the Church who has blessed and guided __________________ will continue to bless, guide, and prosper its legacy.

C) A quiet, private celebration

When only a few members remain and out-of-town guests are not available, the closing service might best be held as a quiet, private celebration.

Prelude

Welcome (No real need to explain the special nature of this service)

Call to Worship

Invocation/Opening Prayer (Focus this prayer as one of thanksgiving for the life and ministry of the church.)

Congregational Music (Selections could be those favorite songs of the congregation or could be selected to focus on the goodness and greatness of God. Possible hymns might include: "Great Is Thy Faithfulness", "How Great Thou Art", "All the Way My Savior Leads Me", "This Is My Father's World"

A Testimony to the Impact of this Church (Those present might be asked to share spontaneously or individuals may be selected in advance. It might also be possible to share a note from a former member.)

A Brief History of the Church (This should be no more than 3–5 minutes.)

Special Music or a Congregational Hymn

Sermon (The sermon should focus on the ongoing mission of the church and could develop the theme of partnership in the larger mission as outlined in Philippians 1.)

Becoming a Legacy Church (A leader from the congregation should explain the decision of the church to continue its legacy and should indicate how that legacy will be realized.)

Accepting the Legacy (If a representative of the denomination is present, appropriate words of commendation and acceptance could be shared with the congregation.)

Candlelight Service – (It may seem a little out of place, but helping a hurting congregation celebrate and focus on the light of Jesus may help to bring closure much like a candlelight vigil held for dead family members.)

Closing Prayer (Led by the denominational representative who will invite the remaining members to come forward for this prayer time.)

The Final Benediction: Inasmuch as the congregation of ____________________ has chosen to end its public ministry and to continue that ministry through conveying it assets to ___________________________, I therefore declare that the public ministry of ______________________ has come to an end and that all remaining legal affairs of the congregation will be entrusted to the congregational leaders in keeping with the previous decision of the church. We give thanks to God for His grace that has blessed ___________________ with an effective ministry. We commend to Him the legacy bestowed this day by _________________ and we ask that the Lord of the Church who has blessed and guided _________________ will continue to bless, guide, and prosper its legacy.

Please remember, to leave a legacy is to pass on to future generations something of great significance. Leaving a legacy should be the hope of every church. If your church can give birth to a new church, that new church can carry your values and beliefs and continue to fulfill your mission to bring life-change to the community. May God grant you wisdom and courage as you consider the pathway of becoming a Legacy church.

APPENDIX I

A Word to Denominational Leaders

Much of what was stated within this book was written with a system of congregational government in mind. We realize that thousands of churches within the United States, operate in denominational systems that do not allow congregations to make the final decision about closure. In these cases, denominational, local association, or district leaders make all the final decisions. If you are like most denominational leaders in the United States you are faced with the unwanted realization that many of your churches will close over the next decade. Let us offer a few suggestions as you journey down this road.

1. Evaluate churches honestly and be bold.

Honest evaluation is difficult. Many leaders are under pressure to report strong progress and an increase in numbers. Closing a church is the last thing you may want to do because it simply doesn't look good. However, honesty is always the best policy. Too many leaders have been avoiding the truth of the situation. It may be hard, but take an honest look at the churches you lead. Are they truly Kingdom churches and do they honestly have a chance of survival? Naturally, we want to say, "YES!" But if we never get brutally honest about our present situation, we will never be able to get beyond it.

In the movie *Harry Potter and the Goblet of Fire*, Professor Dumbledore said to Harry, "There will come a time when people will do what's easy instead of what's right." Does that sound at all familiar to you? Regardless of your opinion of the movie, the statement is sound. Keeping a failing, declining church open may be the easiest path to follow, but is it the *right* path to follow? What is best for the Kingdom of God? Strong, godly leadership requires us to make hard decisions.

We live in a culture that celebrates winners and despises losers. As leaders we can't afford to let that secular mind-set govern our decisions. While many community churches have to be closed, God's kingdom, His Church, will never be silenced.

2. Develop a closure process.

It's really not a matter of "if," but "when." Every church will eventually close. The churches in Acts were no exception. The question is: Will you be reactive or proactive? As the old saying goes, "Failing to plan is planning to fail." Take the time to develop a closure process that will enable the development of new churches through the assets of those that are closing. In this way, the history and vision of every church is honored. A strong process governing church closure can help catapult your association, district, or denomination forward with the gospel of Christ. Don't allow the assets of closing churches to be frittered away or stockpiled for a rainy day. God doesn't need us to bury those talents, but to use them.

3. Honor the historic vision of the church.

Closing a church is painful. There is no way around it. The people in the pews, who have sacrificed and supported this failing ministry, feel demoralized, frustrated, and oftentimes angry. In denominational structures where the congregation has little power or say over closure, the congregation's emotional state can be even worse. We believe it is very important for the congregation to realize that their hard work and sacrifice will not end upon closure. Rather, it will live on through the development of several new congregations. The closing of one church can often provide enough capital to start several new ones. Help the congregation see that closure is not the end, but a new beginning. Assure the congregation that their dream will live on.

4. Constantly cast a vision for legacy churches.

Changing the culture of churches when your organization is bent on survival will take time. So, talk about legacy churches as often as you can. Cast the vision for this process at every public meeting or gathering. Share with your district, association, or denomination a new strategy for funding the start of new churches. Vision will take a while to take hold, so never stop talking about it. About the time you are sick of saying it, everyone else is just beginning to get it.

5. Celebrate legacy churches openly!

We become what we celebrate. Don't let the passing of a church go unnoticed or uncelebrated, especially if the church leaves a legacy. The Christian world is very good at correcting, asking, and teaching, but very poor at celebrating. Don't allow a closing church to go silently into that dark night. At your annual conventions, district meetings, or national gatherings, take time to celebrate the historic impact of a closing church and the potential future through leaving a legacy. Praise the remaining leaders for their faithfulness and sacrifice. Risk and hard work for the Kingdom of God should be celebrated not brushed under the carpet. Celebration of this kind will create a more positive and open atmosphere of hope among the churches you supervise.

6. Allow the local congregation to be part of the decision.

Guide the local church in making good decisions about the placement of the church's assets, but allow them to be a part of the process. By allowing the congregation to own responsibility for the future, you can create a stronger sense of buy-in. Buy-in is extremely important to any movement. Strong buy-in from closing churches will create momentum and maintain a positive sense of direction. You may even find that members from a closing church will become your best advocates for leaving a legacy. Empower and guide your churches to make good, Kingdom-minded decisions and you will reap the benefits.

By contrast, strong-arm tactics and dictatorial edicts produce ill will, frustration, and even a sense of rebellion. The negative momentum from this attitude will be difficult to overcome.

APPENDIX II

Frequently Asked Questions

1. How do you know that all churches go through the organizational life cycle?

Looking back over the history of many, many congregations we can illustrate the principles of the life cycle. A few notable illustrations of these principles can be found by reviewing the history of the Metropolitan Tabernacle in London, Westminster Chapel also in London, and The Church of the Open Door in Los Angeles. Each of these high profile congregations illustrates the transition from birth to growth to maturity and plateau, followed by decline and drop-out. Each of these churches still exists. None of them, however, has yet recovered to the size they were at their heights.

Every church will move through the life cycle stages. Hopefully, with a new awareness of the process, more and more churches will take steps reverse that process as they reach maturity and plateau. This will allow them to move into a new cycle of growth before their energies are sapped by decline and drop-out.

For more reading on this life-cycle we recommend:

- ▲ David T. Olson, The American Church in Crisis: Groundbreaking Research Based on a National Database of over 200,000 Churches (Grand Rapids: Zondervan, 2008).
- ▲ Gary L. McIntosh, One Size Doesn't Fit All: Bringing Out the Best in Any Size Church (Grand Rapids: Revell, 2004).
- ▲ Arnold L. Cook, Historical Drift: Must My Church Die? (Camp Hill: Christian Publications Inc. 2000).

2. Can life cycle stages be reversed?

Yes. Life cycle stages can sometimes be reversed. A large number of denominational offices and para-church organizations now offer services designed to assist churches to refocus and/or restart. However, two items of concern must be noted.

First: The later a church is in the life cycle, the more difficult it is to refocus and/or restart. Those churches near the end of their life cycles find it next to impossible.

Second: Most churches that reverse their life cycle trends do so when the pain of staying the same is greater than the pain of change. Only with a willing spirit and an open mind will a congregation begin to experience the winds of change. Often, current ministry styles of a declining church are not conducive to reverse life cycle stages.

If your church is looking for help or seeking to understand how your life-cycle process might be reversed go to *www.legacychurches.com* for more information.

3. When I review the attendance trends of our church, how do I distinguish between the mature stage and the plateau stage?

Maturity will generally be recognized as the peak or all-time high for the church. All the ministries of the church are working well, finances are excellent, and the sky seems to be the limit. The early stages of plateau are really just the extension of maturity. As this extension continues, either a new growth cycle is developed or the congregation becomes very comfortable with the status quo. In a living organism like the church, to maintain the status quo for an extended time results in the loss of that drive and vision that sees the sky as the limit. A dullness and routine sameness creeps in when the church is on a plateau. Sustained maturity will show statistically as a leveling off or a plateau. Long before the statistical plateau is evidenced, however, there will be a shift in attitudes that can be labeled as a plateau.

4. Our attendance trends are down this year. What level of decline merits concern?

Attendance records can be monitored too closely and can often be taken out of context. This obsession with detail is not frequent, as churches often tend to rationalize or even ignore attendance trends. Decline merits concern if it jeopardizes the life and ministry of the church. Decline merits concern if other churches in the same context are not showing similar decline. Decline also merits concern if this is a sustained decline that can be measured across two or three years. Any such decline should always motivate church leaders to evaluate external and internal factors that might be contributing to the decline.

5. How do we go about listing church real estate for sale?

Church real estate may be listed in much the same fashion as any other real estate. The nature of the property and any zoning restrictions may determine whether a commercial or residential sale is anticipated. Sale of real estate will require action by the congregation to authorize the sale and to execute legal transfer of title.

6. Are there businesses or agencies that specialize in the sale of church property?

Although at least 3,000 churches close annually, we are not aware of agencies that specialize in the sale of church properties. Real estate may be listed with a commercial realtor if the church facility will be used as a church or business property. It is sometimes possible to work with an auction service to sell church property. If the fixtures and furnishings are valuable as antiques, interior decorators and antique dealers may be able to assist.

7. How do we determine the fair market value of an item in the church?

Determining fair market value can be time consuming and a little tricky. Check in your local yellow pages to see if property appraisal companies are in your community. We would recommend that you find a good Christian attorney to help guide you through this process. Make sure they are familiar with Estate law.

If you choose to do without an attorney, consider these factors when placing fair value on an item:

- ▲ What is a buyer willing to pay?
- ▲ What was the original cost of the item?
- ▲ Has the item depreciated or appreciated?
- ▲ What have other, similar items sold for?
- ▲ What are the opinions of experts?

For more information on finding the fair market value of donated property, go to the IRS website. *http://www.irs.gov/publications/p561/ar02.html#d0e139*

8. When I am asked to sign legal documents for my church I am always concerned about the personal liability I may be assuming. Should I be concerned?

When an officer or agent of the church acts in that capacity, he/she is acting for the group and not as an individual. This limited liability is one advantage of being incorporated under the laws of the state. Further, most property insurance policies will have an option to cover directors and officers when they act as agents of the corporation. Generally, legal documents will require that a corporate resolution be included to identify who may sign, and how and when the decision was made authorizing them as agents of the corporation.

9. Only a few of us are left in the church and none of us feels qualified to conduct our final meeting. What options do we have?

One option would be to work with your denominational officials. If your church operates on a congregational system, you may delegate to one of those officials the right to act as convening moderator.

Another option would be to work with an attorney to organize the final meeting in keeping with the laws of the state.

An option that should be avoided is the option to just do nothing because no one feels qualified to act. Doing nothing as the church approaches closure only clouds the issues and makes it all the more likely that the assets of the congregation will not be used constructively.

10. A few members of our church are openly discussing dividing up the furnishings, equipment and fixtures from our historic church after it closes. Is this proper?

If the items in question have no market value, and if the congregation has given permission for such actions, this is proper disposition of church furnishings, fixtures and special memorabilia. If your church is historic, it is very likely that the furnishings, equipment and fixtures do have a fair market value. This fair market value should be determined, and members should then pay that value for the furnishings, equipment and fixtures.

11. The two remaining members of the church are both widowed and have decided that, as members of the church, they are eligible to live in the church-owned parsonage without paying rent. Is this legal?

No. While there is no directly assessed rent, pastors are assessed a fair rental value for the church-owned home. This fair rental value is considered part of their compensation. Even though the pastor pays no rent, the fair market value is reported on the pastor's self employment form as part of standard income tax filings. Individuals who occupy church-owned dwellings would be subject to similar requirements.

APENDIX III

Life Cycle Survey

This survey is a tool to help you gain a quick understanding of where you perceive your church to be in the life cycle. It is not intended to be a definitive tool. For a more in-depth survey of your congregation, please contact us through *www.legacychurches.com*

Step 1. Take the survey. Mark your answers to each question.

Step 2. Transfer the data. Use the number value assigned to each answer and carefully transfer those numbers to indicate your response to each statement.

Step 3. Compute the average response for each column by totaling the responses for each column and dividing by the number of questions/statements included in each category.

Step 4. Note the highest average response and use its column heading to mark your perceived placement of your church on the life cycle chart.

Life Cycle Survey

Life Cycles are more than time lines and attendance statistics. Life Cycles are also measured by attitudes and opinions. The following survey is designed to measure your perception of the congregation's attitudes and opinions. There are no wrong answers, only your answers. Please respond based on your experiences and perceptions about your church. The responses will be collected and tabulated to help identify your church's position on the life cycle.

1. The things we do as a church are done as a result of the driving vision of the senior or lead pastor.

   0. Not at all 1. Once in a while 2. Some of the time 3. Most of the time 4. All the time

2. People come to prayer services when asked to pray for the church.

   0. Not at all 1. Once in a while 2. Some of the time 3. Most of the time 4. All the time

3. The church has a successful ministry with a clear vision for a positive future.

   0. Not at all 1. Once in a while 2. Some of the time 3. Most of the time 4. All the time

4. No specific vision or direction drives the ministries of our church.

   0. Not at all 1. Once in a while 2. Some of the time 3. Most of the time 4. All the time

5. The ministries we do are not done as well as they used to be and our programs are in decline.

   0. Not at all 1. Once in a while 2. Some of the time 3. Most of the time 4. All the time

6. People often quit doing the ministry tasks they initially agreed to do.

   0. Not at all 1. Once in a while 2. Some of the time 3. Most of the time 4. All the time

7. Our church uses our savings to pay the regular bills.

   0. Not at all 1. Once in a while 2. Some of the time 3. Most of the time 4. All the time

8. The atmosphere in the church is one of enthusiasm, and people are passionate about living out their faith and the mission established by the founding members of the church.

   0. Not at all 1. Once in a while 2. Some of the time 3. Most of the time 4. All the time

9. Outreach is obvious and new people regularly come into the life and ministries of the church.

   0. Not at all 1. Once in a while 2. Some of the time 3. Most of the time 4. All the time

10. Overall, the church feels it is at its strongest point and has the resources to accomplish a great deal.

0. Not at all 1. Once in a while 2. Some of the time 3. Most of the time 4. All the time

11. People are passive and apathetic about the church.

0. Not at all 1. Once in a while 2. Some of the time 3. Most of the time 4. All the time

12. People like to talk about the good old days and it seems that our best days are behind us.

0. Not at all 1. Once in a while 2. Some of the time 3. Most of the time 4. All the time

13. Ministry positions often go unfilled because volunteers are hard to come by.

0. Not at all 1. Once in a while 2. Some of the time 3. Most of the time 4. All the time

14. Our church receives outside support to keep the doors open.

0. Not at all 1. Once in a while 2. Some of the time 3. Most of the time 4. All the time

15. We just do ministry with very little organization in place to guide it.

0. Not at all 1. Once in a while 2. Some of the time 3. Most of the time 4. All the time

16. We seem to have a plan to encourage fellowship, develop care ministries, and to train new leaders.

0. Not at all 1. Once in a while 2. Some of the time 3. Most of the time 4. All the time

17. People are active and involved. Spiritual growth is obvious.

0. Not at all 1. Once in a while 2. Some of the time 3. Most of the time 4. All the time

18. Our mission as a church seems to be maintaining what we've got.

0. Not at all 1. Once in a while 2. Some of the time 3. Most of the time 4. All the time

19. We have tended to look for a way to blame our current condition on someone or something else.

0. Not at all 1. Once in a while 2. Some of the time 3. Most of the time 4. All the time

20. Our worship services are dominated by memories of the past.

0. Not at all 1. Once in a while 2. Some of the time 3. Most of the time 4. All the time

21. Our pastor used to be full time but has become bivocational.

0. Not at all 1. Once in a while 2. Some of the time 3. Most of the time 4. All the time

22. Congregational members often wonder "Who are we?" as a church.

0. Not at all 1. Once in a while 2. Some of the time 3. Most of the time 4. All the time

23. The people of the church live consistent with what the church believes and teaches.

0. Not at all 1. Once in a while 2. Some of the time 3. Most of the time 4. All the time

24. Worship services are enthusiastic and enjoyed by all. They are highly rated by all who attend.

0. Not at all 1. Once in a while 2. Some of the time 3. Most of the time 4. All the time

25. We do very few new things if there is a chance they might fail.

0. Not at all 1. Once in a while 2. Some of the time 3. Most of the time 4. All the time

26. Church income is low.

0. Not at all 1. Once in a while 2. Some of the time 3. Most of the time 4. All the time

27. We are hesitant to take risks that might use all the resources we have.

0. Not at all 1. Once in a while 2. Some of the time 3. Most of the time 4. All the time

28. Our morale is low.

0. Not at all 1. Once in a while 2. Some of the time 3. Most of the time 4. All the time

29. We often talk about our need for a new building to house our growing ministries.

0. Not at all 1. Once in a while 2. Some of the time 3. Most of the time 4. All the time

30. Our worship services are done in a style that fits us and provides an inspirational high point.

0. Not at all 1. Once in a while 2. Some of the time 3. Most of the time 4. All the time

31. We are looking forward to the future.

0. Not at all 1. Once in a while 2. Some of the time 3. Most of the time 4. All the time

32. What we are doing as a church is working.

0. Not at all 1. Once in a while 2. Some of the time 3. Most of the time 4. All the time

33. We really need something new.

0. Not at all 1. Once in a while 2. Some of the time 3. Most of the time 4. All the time

34. Our nursing home list is long, and funerals are frequent.

0. Not at all 1. Once in a while 2. Some of the time 3. Most of the time 4. All the time

35. We are not looking forward to the future; there is little hope for us.

0. Not at all 1. Once in a while 2. Some of the time 3. Most of the time 4. All the time

36. People serve in the areas where they have spiritual gifts and active interest.

0. Not at all 1. Once in a while 2. Some of the time 3. Most of the time 4. All the time

37. Church income is high.

0. Not at all 1. Once in a while 2. Some of the time 3. Most of the time 4. All the time

38. Everything is O.K. so we do not need to change or adapt.

0. Not at all 1. Once in a while 2. Some of the time 3. Most of the time 4. All the time

39. The number of people who leave our church is greater than the new ones who join.

0. Not at all 1. Once in a while 2. Some of the time 3. Most of the time 4. All the time

40. People no longer invite others to our worship services.

0. Not at all 1. Once in a while 2. Some of the time 3. Most of the time 4. All the time

41. We often talk about how to keep the doors open.

0. Not at all 1. Once in a while 2. Some of the time 3. Most of the time 4. All the time

42. We have healthy, inspirational worship, consistent outreach and we are making disciples.

0. Not at all 1. Once in a while 2. Some of the time 3. Most of the time 4. All the time

43. Attendance is higher than it has ever been.

0. Not at all 1. Once in a while 2. Some of the time 3. Most of the time 4. All the time

44. The folks who attend our church have all attended faithfully for some time.

0. Not at all 1. Once in a while 2. Some of the time 3. Most of the time 4. All the time

45. Overall, our church shows the beginning signs of aging.

0. Not at all 1. Once in a while 2. Some of the time 3. Most of the time 4. All the time

46. Our church is a preaching point; we do little else beyond weekly worship.

0. Not at all 1. Once in a while 2. Some of the time 3. Most of the time 4. All the time

47. Our church has several new believers but no discipleship plan for them.

0. Not at all 1. Once in a while 2. Some of the time 3. Most of the time 4. All the time

48. The things we are doing in ministry are working better than ever before.

0. Not at all 1. Once in a while 2. Some of the time 3. Most of the time 4. All the time

49. We have fewer children and teens than we used to have.

0. Not at all 1. Once in a while 2. Some of the time 3. Most of the time 4. All the time

50. We have more senior citizens than any other age group.

0. Not at all 1. Once in a while 2. Some of the time 3. Most of the time 4. All the time

51. People in the community know who we are as a church.

0. Not at all 1. Once in a while 2. Some of the time 3. Most of the time 4. All the time

52. We don't get along well and our personal relationships are often strained.

0. Not at all 1. Once in a while 2. Some of the time 3. Most of the time 4. All the time

53. We often talk about the way things used to be.

0. Not at all 1. Once in a while 2. Some of the time 3. Most of the time 4. All the time

54. Our system of making decisions and keeping the church organized is working well.

0. Not at all 1. Once in a while 2. Some of the time 3. Most of the time 4. All the time

55. Some groups in the church suffer from low morale.

0. Not at all 1. Once in a while 2. Some of the time 3. Most of the time 4. All the time

Life Cycle Stages							
	Birth	Growth	Maturity	Plateau	Decline	Dropout	Death
Responses	1	2	3	4	5	6	7
for each	8	9	10	11	12	13	14
item	15	16	17	18	19	20	21
	22	23	24	25	26	27	28
	29	30	31	32	33	34	35
		36	37	38	39	40	41
		42	43	44		45	46
		47	48			49	50
			51			52	53
			54				55
Responses Totaled by Column l							
Divided by	5	8	10	7	6	9	10
Average Score							

atkins.com